101 Tales of Finding Love

Volume One

COMPILED AND EDITED BY

IRMA SHEPPARD

Table Of Contents

Dedicated to Avatar Meher Baba
whose continuing manifestation
lights our hearts
one by one by one.

The Game

To penetrate into the essence
of all being and significance,
and to release the fragrance
of that inner attainment for
the guidance of others,
by expressing in
the world of forms -
truth, love, purity, and beauty -
this is the sole game which has any
intrinsic and absolute worth.
All other happenings,
incidents and attainments can,
in themselves,
have no lasting importance.

~ Avatar Meher Baba

Introduction

In December 2016, during a break in Ward Parks' seminar on *Stay with God*, I heard a woman's story of how she came to Meher Baba. I was struck by the singularity of the events that drew her to experience Baba's love. It occurred to me that our stories of how He prepares us to receive His love, to accept Him as God in human form, the Avatar of the age, are invaluable to each of us and to those who will come after us.

These stories speak for themselves.

I am truly grateful to each of these contributors for recollecting their profound and heartfelt experiences of finding Love, writing them down and sending them for inclusion in this book.

Several of the contributors to this collection of stories told me how meaningful the process was of gathering their thoughts and memories, and reliving that time of unutterable joy—finding themselves internally present with Him, the Beloved of all.

In His Abiding Love,
Irma Sheppard
Asheville, North Carolina
irmasheppard@icloud.com
June 13, 2017

P.S. Thirty-seven years ago today, I stepped into my first Meher Baba meeting in Los Angeles. I remember standing at the threshold, thinking, "This is the place."

Aug 1, 2019

For my dear friend,
        Sharon,

There is light at
the end of the tunnel,
and you have the <u>Friend</u>
to guide you through
the dark places, to hold
your hand, and pull
you out the other
side.

        Much love + Light,
        Jackie Boyce Aug 2019

Foreword

I was so pleased when my dear friend Irma asked me to be part of introducing this book to you. It's a project I've been enthusiastic about since the first time she shared the idea with me.

Here we find a new collection of stories of how people found the love and compassion of the Avatar of the age, Meher Baba. The tales have been submitted from Baba's lovers spanning the world, each with a unique path leading to his feet; each with a stirring story to tell.

Irma and her husband Karl Moeller make a gifted team, with years of experience both in writing and publishing, and in their many years loving their Master, Meher Baba. The result is a striking volume both in its pleasing layout and design, and in the skilled editing in which each writer's individual voice is retained.

There have been numerous collections of this nature published, with heart-warming tales to tell. Yet this new collection has merit in the breadth of its sources and in the attractive visual form it takes.

Irma continues to collect stories and plans additional volumes until she fulfills the title's theme: 101 tales of finding love.

Winnie Barrett
Asheville, NC
July, 2017

Artwork © Claire Mataira

101 Tales
of Finding Love

THE MIRACLE
OF SURRENDERING

by Jan Baker

My story of coming to Baba unfolded retrospectively over thirty-one years. It unconsciously began on 30th May 1978.

Since childhood I had a burning passion to get to India, having been brought up on exotic, romantic and terrifying tales from my great aunt who'd grown up there in the times of the Raj. After saving for some years, a girlfriend and I determined to travel overland through Europe, Turkey, Iran, Afghanistan and Pakistan.

Before committing to Asia we'd decided to spend time in Israel. In the 1970s many travellers would migrate there to work on a Kibbutz as it was regarded a safe place to hold up, seek travelling companions, await funds from home or work to finance further travels.

Subsequently we'd met up with two Canadians who were likewise looking to get to India (Peter, a down-to-earth seasoned traveller and Barbara, a somewhat hysterical eccentric seeking adventure). Because of visa complications in Turkey, our group became divided and I found myself continuing onward and beyond with Barbara and two acquaintances she'd met over Turkish tea, whom she enthused were God-sent and would make perfect travelling companions-cum-chaperones named Mohander and Jit. They were driving back overland to Delhi and would be very happy to share costs and enjoy our company.

Over the three days we travelled together it transpired that Mohander, the dominant of the two friends, was from a wealthy Indian family, involved in the film business and purported to be close friends of the Gandhi dynasty.

On the fourth day the car broke down—fortunately near enough to push to the next village. Mohander and I checked into a cheap hotel whilst Jit went in search of a garage and Barbara a post office.

Having checked into a hotel, I unpacked and decided to take a much needed shower. After just a few moments Mohander began insistently banging on the flimsy bathroom door, and when I refused to open it, forced the lock and pinned me to the wall.

When danger hits, the mind accelerates beyond the senses, assessing in seconds all available options of flight or fight. In my case, as each was tried or tested and proved futile there came a point when I knew that the only one left was surrender, if I was to survive.

And then something quite incredible happened. I found myself floating outside of my body and looking down on the scene from the small makeshift balcony outside of the room. I didn't feel at all scared. In fact I remember wondering if perhaps I should simply continue to float away, when two lengths of toilet paper caught my attention. They'd become caught in the balcony railings and I became riveted by their graceful movements, and as they danced in the wind they communicated to me that I was also and would ever be free just like them—that whatever was happening to the body lying beneath could never harm or corrupt that which was really me. So I simply waited for the assault to be concluded, like witnessing a story already written, before returning and burying the whole incident in a deep place and taping it closed.

The shock from this attack propelled me through the intervening countries. Mindful of staying safe in such politically turbulent times, I was also intuitively aware that I was now being accompanied and cared for by an invisible presence.

Such is the irony of life, when our purported protectors become our persecutors and in turn our liberators. So it was with the passage of time, Mohander's identity and role changed in the bigger picture of my life, from initial escort to assailant to saviour. He was my first thread to Meher Baba, with his actions taking on some of my sanskaric debris that may have also helped in my awareness of Baba's presence.

In each major city or stopover we'd be met with a physical protector as well. In Mashhad we were literally pulled off the streets and invited into a family home to stay until it was deemed safe enough to resume our journey. During our time with them they insisted on taking us to the Blue Mosque, lending us clothes to avoid unwanted attention and impressing on us its spiritual importance and their belief that "as travellers you are messengers from Allah." (Of course, later learning of Baba's vigil inside this very mosque, it seemed like another Hansel and Gretel bread crumb in my real journey home.)

Some three months later, 23rd August, I was staying with a small fishing community on the outskirts of Puri, on route to Poona (Pune). The following day was to be my birthday, but I was awoken in the early hours of that morning with severe stomach pains. Sitting up I was shocked to see a pool of blood which had collected in my lap. It seems incredible now that the concept of pregnancy from the assault hadn't once dawned on me, but my diary simply reads that this was my birthday present from God, and that its overdue arrival was down to the amount of fear and tension that my body was carrying.

On 27th August I spent the night on the platform of Poona railway station in between connections—such a brief period of time but it inexplicably made an indelible impression. From here my travels took me all over India and Sri Lanka until funds ran low and suffering ill health I was forced to return overland back to the United Kingdom. I'd been away for fourteen months.

My initial re-entry into the West was not easy, with its associated materialism and perceived shallowness of soul standing in stark contrast to the depth of Eastern spirituality. I reacted by turning my frustrations in on myself, creating a self-destructive edge until my passions wore thin enough for me to settle for floating on life's surface. That is, until I met and fell in love with my future husband, Brian Gordon Baker.

Brian was both sensitive, exceedingly funny and gifted with psychical insight, but this was counter-balanced with a history of mental ill health and addiction. He was also the only soul I had met who shared my spiritual beliefs.

Following the births of our children we made the conscious decision to turn our backs on consumerism and conformity and bought a derelict cottage in the country where we could be as self-sufficient as life in the West allowed and not be governed by the nine-to-five norm of society. I'd literally been given an incredible job not so long after my return from travelling, at Trinity College, Cambridge. As well as a very healthy salary, the position came with an interest free mortgage allowing us to buy our own house. This in turn had appreciated so much during my years with them that we came away with over £65,000 to invest in a new life style.

Unfortunately, as time progressed and my attention became more directed toward the children's lives and my own emotional growth, Brian's paranoia and alcoholism grew also. When it began to seriously threaten my mental health, and after exhausting all alternatives over the years, I decided to take the children and flee. Over the ensuing months and then years of separation, threats and fears, the invisible protective presence that had made itself felt during my earlier travels never once left me. It was also accompanied by the emergence of an internal voice of overwhelming knowing. Far more insistent than my fear was the recognised wisdom that my responses must always come from a place of love. This was pretty much all I was sure of during this time. My sense of self and reality had been so eroded that all I had was this intuitive knowledge that, if honoured, would safeguard us all. Incredibly, all the practicalities like work, house and money were taken care of by, as I believed it, God. So many little miracles happened over this resettlement period. As each new threat appeared, it was met and dealt with without any conscious actions from myself, as if our little boat were being steered by an all-knowing, all-powerful hand.

Fear is surely the most destructive and distortive of forces and when combined with mental ill health, drugs and alcohol it can gnaw at and ultimately dissolve the very core and fabric of a heart. In this desperate state of being and abandonment and unable to reach me physically, Brian would threaten to haunt me at night in his astral body. Seeking protection I approached a wise healer friend and underwent the three courses of Reiki attunements. This all may appear quite hysterical behaviour, and perhaps it was, but at the time my reality had become completely detached and merged into the night-and-daymare of Brian's existence. It was an all-consuming realm of shadows and fear, and quite terrifyingly illustrated the very fine mental membrane which divides each of our worlds.

Reminiscent of the scene in "The Matrix" when Morpheus offers Leo the choice of ingesting the blue or the red capsule determining entry into a new paradigm, Liz (my healer and friend) cautioned me that the final attunement would adjust my psychic frequencies making me both more sensitive and attractive to subtle energies and in turn, fundamentally alter my sense of reality.

Shortly after this we went to stay with my parents on the outskirts of St. Albans. I'd accompanied my mum into town and was waiting for her in the main Post Office when my arm was tapped by a hunchbacked man in rather shabby clothes. Turning to face him I felt a deep recognition although I'd consciously never met him before. Unable to speak, he began murmuring the soft letter *d* and pointing to two blank post cards on a side counter. After some time I guessed that the word he was trying to communicate was "date" and he instantly guided me to the two cards and motioned me to write that day's date at the top of each one. A few minutes later he tapped me again and began making the sound "haw haw." By this time Mum had joined us and she too was attempting to understand what he was trying to say. He was becoming more and more agitated and shaking as if in fear. I finally said the word "haunt" to which he smiled and again led me to the two cards.

Underneath the date he'd written in block letters:

DEAR LIZ,
NEVER NEVER
NEVER NEVER
NEVER NEVER LIE

 He indicated for me to write the word "haunt" in the space below, and beneath this was Brian's signature. In a state of amazement I obeyed, simply trusting it to be the right and seemingly normal thing to do. He then tapped my arm again, opened his jacket and pulled out his wallet. Unfolding it he showed me a card upon which was emblazoned:

"Always look on the bright side of life."

This was our little mantra—whenever my mum phoned during times of stress we would sing this and it would automatically lift our spirits and allow us to simply laugh our fears away. Carefully folding and placing the wallet back into his jacket he smiled, said a clear "good bye" and walked away. I became more and more convinced that this strange contact had been an angel as my life began to change and Brian's threats and accusations began to boomerang back onto him. He finally moved away to Newton Abbot, Devon, oddly enough, into a house opposite one I'd rented in my youth, long before we'd met.

Seeking a sense of grounding and normality and also a sense of self, I took a two-year Higher National Diploma course in Performing Arts but despite playing, exploring and being so many differing characters, the question "Who am I?" began to dominate my thinking more and more. I knew who I wasn't, and couldn't understand how everyone else seemed to have an identity but me. I decided to compose a letter to a very old friend, convinced he could help me find it.

Whilst crossing the street to post this letter I was intercepted by a woman getting out of a large American car who asked if she could talk with me. Now please understand that Clun, where we were then living, had been pickled in aspic since the Middle Ages, being perfectly summed up in Houseman's famous poem as being the "quietest place under the sun." Indeed, when we'd first arrived, the novelty of "folk from off" would attract a crowd of inquisitive locals, so the presence of an American car, let alone its flamboyant occupant was most definitely not the norm. It transpired that she'd just flown over from the States due to an inheritance and was on her way back when she'd been intuitively led through the Clun valley, as she explained to me.

She was a follower of Osho and she'd been living in Poona in 1978, when I'd spent those hours on the platform at Poona train station. She explained that she was looking to invest this inheritance in buying a tea room in the United Kingdom with the focus on laughter—to create a cheerful atmosphere of joy and simplicity to nourish the heart as well as the stomach. Should she find the right place she would like me to manage it. Such synchronicity didn't go un-noted: that I was currently helping run the village tea rooms which the owner had literally just decided to sell, that my studies had most recently led me into laughter therapy, and that the friend to whom I'd just written had been an Osho disciple.

Although I didn't see this woman again, she left me with a comforting assurance that I was not alone on this strange journey, an affirmation of the healing properties of laughter (of which I knew my sanity was testament) and that Poona was somehow significant.

Not so long after this encounter, a close friend and Baba lover, Fiona Robertson, telephoned, inviting me to join her in going to Poona, India and I immediately agreed. I'd first become acquainted with Fiona some years prior through three independent mediums—fund raising, spirituality and work, so I guess our friendship was pretty unavoidable.

The first time I heard Meher Baba's name was at Fiona's first attendance at a spiritual group meeting where she showed a Baba film and gave an introductory talk. Although I warmed to Him I was very guarded.

As our friendship grew she would often mention His name but I remained resistant of becoming a "follower" of any particular master. Indeed, if she'd suggested going to India for Baba-related reasons I really don't know if I'd have gone, but she didn't and all I heard was Poona, and that was the hook.

As soon as we arrived in this place of Baba's birth I felt both at home and in love, and in response my heart began to soften. And so it was that we progressed to Meherabad.

This was January 2009 and Meherabad was gearing up for Amartithi. On my first day I decided to explore the small village of Arangaon, partly to get away on my own and partly to rekindle my love of simple India. No one had advised against or told me of the potential dangers and so I sauntered off with camera to acquaint myself with and capture village life.

Within minutes of arrival I was approached from opposite directions by two snarling dogs, and on turning felt a sudden sharp stab at the back of my leg. Thinking I'd been hit by a stone I was shocked to discover my shoe filling with blood from an obvious bite and then villagers shouting and coming to my rescue. There followed a series of rabies injections, but far more disquieting was my new attraction and relationship with dogs. Each time I ventured out of the pilgrim centre, I would be met with either one dog or a pack of snarling aggression. Such internal churnings were now taking place that I was advised to seek the council of Bob Street, Meherabad's resident homeopath. Looking back, I believe that first shock helped dislodge historically repressed fears and then literally talking them out released them into the light of consciousness. Sitting daily in Baba's Samadhi I physically felt the waves of His love washing over and into these ingrained stains that had hitherto taken such deep rooted residence in my heart.

Looking back I am in absolutely no doubt that the protective presence I first became aware of in 1978 and which had accompanied me during those most fearful times was none other than Baba. So many internal revelations and external co-incidences have unfolded since then to confirm and corroborate this beyond question.

Likewise, the voice that guided me away from fear, to trust in love I believe was His—manifesting through my heart and accompanied by so powerful a knowing that it was impossible to ignore or suppress. A merger of feeling and hearing, of His voice and my voice, so that I couldn't distinguish betwixt, but which made it all the more truthful, trustful and commanding.

That it took half a lifetime of fear to prompt that one primal question, "Who am I?" and in turn prime my heart to finally recognise and receive Him is not only testament to His unfathomable patience but also His unwavering love. To constantly and consistently believe in me until the time was ripe for me to believe in Him.

In 2015 Baba turned the key and after sixteen years of sufferance, all of Brian's anger and resentment toward me miraculously dissolved and I recognised the beautiful man I'd first fallen in love with. Just over three weeks later I telephoned him from Baba's tomb to ask if he'd like to take darshan with me but there was no reply so I left a voicemail. We don't know the exact time he passed away but a neighbour discovered him around midday. It was 19th September, during the ten day festivity of Ganesh, the dissolver of all obstacles.

*****

I currently work with laughter and exercise for the elderly and live near St Albans, Hertfordshire, England, with my daughter, two cocker spaniels and one Persian cat.

101 Tales
of Finding Love

FINDING REAL LOVE

by Paula Baran

Artwork © Claire Mataira

y first visit to the Meher Spiritual Center in Myrtle Beach was in January 2014. I knew nothing about the Center except that it was a beautiful old retreat. I knew nothing about Meher Baba, but was told anyone could go there for a spiritual retreat and you would not be required to drink the kool aid (not required to believe in Baba). It seemed amazing that there was an Indian teacher who had developed a retreat in Myrtle Beach, a two-hour drive from my home in central North Carolina. I had dreamed of going to India to study wisdom teachings. Starting close to home seemed like a good beginning.

In 2008 my family and I moved to North Carolina. My husband had cancer and wanted to be near his family. We had lived in Alabama near my family. Life can change in a minute, we learned with a cancer diagnosis. I had just retired, had my first horse in many years, lived in the perfect place with my people. I thought I had worked hard to earn this perfect retirement, but it was not to be. We left Birmingham, could not sell our house, but bought a small farm in Southern Pines, North Carolina. My husband could not work so I had to go back to work teaching. Our daughter, entering high school when we moved, was very gracious and willing to do anything that might help her father survive. Two years later he died.

Many thought we would return to Alabama after my husband passed, but there was no going back. Like they say, the river moves on and you can not step back into the same river you stepped out of. I did not want to move our daughter again. She had been supported through a difficult time by friends and family in North Carolina. Two years later she received a full scholarship to engineering school at East Carolina University.

Left on the farm with no family, I was very lonely. It was the first time I had ever really lived alone. After two years by myself on the farm and still floundering, unable to find what to do with myself, I hired a life coach, Glenn Fox. He was an angel and encouraged me to get my life together in all the ways I had neglected while having a family. He also encouraged me to go to the Baba Center for a Spiritual Retreat.

January 25, 2014 I made my first trip to the center. When I was being shown around I was invited by Jeff Wolverton to join the few others at the center for a birthday party. José, the honoree, a man who had come to the center for a quiet retreat on his seventieth birthday, was also a first timer and also knew little about Baba. The party was amazing. Jeff and Annie were the hosts of the party. Jeff had cards with famous sayings that he loved written on them. He told us we could look through and pick a card and read it to José for his birthday gift. It turned out to be an amazing party—everyone reading their cards to José was beautiful. Annie made a cake with seventy candles all lit in a blaze, and in one breath José blew them all out. I was impressed with the beautiful place, the lovely people, and it was my first afternoon at the center. I felt a sweetness that I had never experienced before.

José explained at the party that he had lost his daughter to cancer the previous year. He'd moved to Asheville to retire with his wife of thirty-five years when his daughter from his first marriage got sick. He returned to California to care for her. He said it was a great gift to be with her but it had taken a toll on his life. Her several years' struggle with cancer was instrumental in ending his marriage. Now he too was alone and a seeker. His story seemed all so familiar and so sad.

That evening, my only evening at the Center, I went to the movie they were showing about Baba. I love everything Indian and went for the old movies and tried to understand this Baba story. José came in and sat down beside me. After the movie we talked and he asked me what I thought about the Avatar stuff. We both agreed it was over the top. This Indian man saying he is God? But we also agreed that there was something special about Baba and this Center. The movies enchanted me—and that enchantment spread out to the place, the time, the people and José.

I was leaving the next day, but José was there for several more days. I invited him to breakfast with me the next morning and we stayed a long time sharing our spiritual and family histories. I had met no one like him and admired the depth of his spiritual knowledge, and his child-like fun nature. He grew up in California in the sixties, meeting many of the spiritual masters that came through. I grew up in Alabama, fending off the Bible beaters, later thinking I wanted to be a Buddhist. I was drawn to this man José, and he to me. I invited him to my farm, saying it was in the middle of the state, and must be on his way back to Asheville. Now that I know how geographically challenged he is, it is a miracle he found me, but three days later he showed up near my house. I passed him on the road (coincidence, we said) and we recognized each other. He was lost but had made it within a few miles of the farm.

I was off work due to my first ever case of pinkeye, interesting I thought—twenty-four hours of no personal contact allowed with anyone. The first man of any interest to me in four years and I could not get too close to him! A snowstorm was predicted for the next day and rumors of a snow day and no school appealed to me—I thought there may be hope! José came with many books on Meher Baba. He had begun reading and felt there may really be something to the Avatar thing. The snowstorm hit and we were snowed in for three days, learning all about each other and Baba. It was beautiful, magical, and very healing for us both. When the snow melted we made two important decisions: we needed to be a couple and there was something powerful with Meher Baba. We knew Baba had brought us together.

José said he would move to the farm. I said, "Heck no!" I wanted to go to Asheville! I told him I would sell the farm and move into his small apartment, which I had never even seen. Downsizing to a three-room apartment seems perfect when you are in love. Our euphoria was powerful and energizing. After many years a great weight was lifted off my shoulders—I had been lost but now I felt found. Our plan was for me to finish out the school year, and he would help me prepare the house and farm for sale. We had a long distance relationship and all went perfectly. The farm sold within a month of being put on the market for the price I wanted. A major miracle—real estate, especially farms, had not been selling except at foreclosure prices. We felt Baba was making it so easy for us.

I moved to Asheville in July of 2014. We had no idea there was such a large Baba community here. We started attending meetings, loved the people we met and the material we were reading. *God Speaks* was our first book group with all the major Asheville Baba scholars in attendance at Elaine's house each week. It just happened to be around the corner from where we lived. That was quite the intro to the Baba community. Cathy and Tom Riley, Peter Nordeen, Bruce Felknor, Gary Kleiner, Winnie Barrett and sometimes Ward Parks. It seemed so beautiful to have all of this. We spent a year of bliss after I moved in, which was very healing for me. I had been so sad for so long that I did not realize how wonderful life could be at my ripe old age of sixty-two. It was a charmed time for my personal and spiritual development.

But while it seemed so perfect, the euphoria eventually wore off and we were just two human beings. I was not a perfect person and neither was he, so after a perfect year we began to see our imperfections. We tried being just friends, living together enjoying the time reading and studying together. But it was not to be. For me there was great sadness again, but this time there was also great anger, probably pent up for most of my life. It all came through the intolerable situation I found myself in. It was as if Kali emerged and cleaned me right out. I felt positively possessed—very, very angry. It was scary for both of us, but in the end I think we both gained a great deal of insight to ourselves that could not have happened any other way.

He is still a Baba lover and so am I. At some level we still love and respect each other and can laugh at ourselves, and even at Kali. It may be that Baba knew we needed each other to get to Him—the Real Love. It was all a wonderful gift and Baba is the Real Love we both get to keep.

Paula Baran

*****

These days I've settled down in Asheville: me, Levi (my dog), Starlite (my horse) and Baba. I bought an old house in town and rent out rooms through Airbnb. It is great fun, I am never lonely, many interesting people from many interesting places show up, stay for a few joy filled days and move on. Baba and I meet them at the door.

101 Tales of Finding Love

THE FIRE OF COMPASSION
(A boy stumbling on the Spiritual Path)

by William Bibby

Artwork © Claire Mataira

William Bibby

Since this memoir is a memory of youth I should begin with the astonishing fact that I was compassionately hauled up out of the ditch by a *complete stranger*, whom I subsequently began to comprehend as God in Human Form, the God Man, *The Divine Enigma*, as Elizabeth Patterson called Him as she beheld Meher Baba for the first time.

THE FIRST ROOM:

> *So. At the bottom of filthy secret stairs in the basement, on a small landing outside an axed door frame and panelled door is a two-ring Belling electric cooker. On the rings, straddling both rings, lies a blackened frying pan and in it bubbles the mud of slowly reducing paragoric. Inside the room three young men dreamily strap their upper arms with belts and thin rubber tubes and almost silent, except for the air, pass the works round, full of blood and opiate. A girl with lank unwashed hair is slapping up the vein in the crook of one of the men's arms. It is cold but everyone is sweating. No one can afford heroin any more. Cough mixture from the chemist is all we can get, reducing it to a brown sludge and pumping it intravenously into our shaking bodies. There is a gust of air from the street as someone enters the hallway above. The door creaks on its shattered hinge. I am coming down the stairs.*

It was a casual and indifferent slide downwards although I didn't know that I was descending. What had happened was I had fallen in love and then discovered that I had fallen through love and had been thrown out the other side. I was nineteen years old and in a sort of numb despair. I didn't even know I was in despair, I didn't know I was falling. I didn't know anything. I was escaping of course, from parents, middle class society—increasingly dismissive of and hurtling toward my own adventure, breathing it all in. I wasn't politically engaged. I didn't want to save anything. I didn't want to save anyone. It was a discreet, almost mechanically incremental, step by hopeless step toward a blank. The 'love' faded into a fog. She had left behind, unwittingly, a landscape of rubble. Thinking of it now I am in awe of the pure elemental power of love, that when it's lost, can strip personality, thought, ideology, of its sinews, its muscle and just leave a skeleton. I tried to kill myself.

I was at Contemporary Film Makers Studios in Kilburn, London, funded by a small allowance from my father nearly all of which went on drugs. The 'room' was off Harrow Road just east of the junction with Ladbroke Grove in Kilburn, opposite the police station. It was February 1969. As well as heroin (or cough mixture or methadone or viceptone) I was taking LSD (more potent than anything available now), sometimes two trips a day and living in a junkie squat in Oxford Gardens with no furniture, bare floor boards and a girl called Ariel who was dying of neglect. We were probably both doing this. I remember the bare light bulb in the flaking ceiling. It was incredibly cold.

We made love not because of any particular affection, although I think we felt sorry for each other, so had a certain empathy, but rather to keep warm. To get some pleasure. To wring out the final pleasures that our bodies could provide.

Thin and with insomnia and the beginnings of chronic, perpetual headaches, I went to the studios after the short break halfway through the course in late February and they made me see a doctor. I went to Dunbar and Hutt on Ladbroke Grove toward the junction with Holland Park. Their surgery was in a crescent. I was given aspirin, Mandrax and cannabis tincture and told to fuck off. Their waiting room was full of smack heads and amphetamine fashion models. The hippy dream!

All this was a huge contrast from the year before. In 1968 I lived in Chelsea, with the Beatles, on the threshold of J. Walter Thompson, in the doorway of Quorum. I was in love, eighteen years old, and had just experienced an impossible thing. Unsayable. With no convincing explanation, but nevertheless it arrived. A moment when it became radiantly clear that the whole world was about to change. That everything was about to lift into light.

Whole continents were about to levitate. It was unbearable, optimistic, full of music and happiness in a kind of virtuous 'now.' I was ecstatic as though some great effulgence had bathed the world in a unifying glory without throwing a shadow. The colours of that year were primary, bright, yielding and joyful. And the year before, 1967, was a miracle of opening doors and looking into other worlds washed with the music of the Beatles and the contact high, as Ian Macdonald put it, with a culture that no one knew existed. Except the music did. And the culture followed on its heels, saturated in drugs.

I made several films at film school, but the one I remember best was shot in an underground car park off Park Lane with two actors. One from the Ballet Rambert and one from Webber Douglas. The central moment in this gritty and ambitiously lit, eight-minute drama was the lead coming face-to-face with himself after having beaten up his girlfriend. So, after destroying his life (and the director of the film wreaking his revenge), he is suddenly confronted by himself. I think I may have been engaged in trying to illustrate someone's predicament, although at the time this eluded me.

Apart from girls, poetry, film and photography and self-destruction, my only other interest was the beginning of a vague recognition that things were not as they seemed. By things I mean the very act of being alive. I wasn't being told something. Something was being hidden from me. This thought became increasingly urgent. I had heard about Zen Buddhism from the poetry of Gary Snyder and also began to read R.H. Blyth's translations of Japanese Haiku. The thought that really caught my attention from about 1966 onwards, which was my last year at school, was "What existed before God?" Or "Who made God?" And more abstractly but with a shudder of presentiment, "What was it that was asking these questions? What am I? What are we? What is I?"

I had, of course, heard about God. Meeting Him first at about six or seven in a visit to the Catholic Cathedral in Perth, Scotland, in the company of my father and god-father. I can't recall why we were there. I bought, for a shilling, a little booklet from the table by the font which contained about four engravings by Gustav Doré. From Dante's *Divine Comedy,* they depicted circle upon circle of angels disappearing in multitudinous hosts, spiralling up into Heaven. I was transported and began to long for this vision. Otherwise I heard rumours of God from red-faced, licentious vicars whose breath smelt of diseased pigs' liver and who ranted about the cauldrons of Hell. As a prep-school boy and then a public (private) school adolescent, I endured this every Sunday for two-thirds of each year at boarding schools for eleven years that I had first attended at the age of six. I did like 'vespers' and loved some of the psalms, which I knew by heart. They were music, but they were not an answer.

Zen came as a totally shocking idea, but one that I soon became comfortable with. That there was a 'nothing' and in that moment was also contained 'everything' made complete sense to me, although it was and is impossible to be articulate about. Nevertheless, reading the poetry of Hart Crane and Whitman I was plunged into an emotive language that swirled and dipped and soared. This was not a very literary analysis of two of America's greatest modern poets but I think the truth was that, when I was introduced by a friend to Ginsberg and Ferlinghetti and Greg Corso, it clarified the world to some extent. There was a clean, empty serenity about this strange Japanese fixation with 'one-pointedness,' and I walked quietly into the echoing temple. I expected boundlessness and a sort of ochre unlimited plain, an actual space, where action had no residual effect upon the actor. But Zen wasn't powerful enough to seduce me away from my self-immolation.

At Contemporary Film Makers Studios were other students. Barry from Australia, who made films of model cardboard sets he built himself, animated by puppets he had constructed. They were incredibly violent. Helena from Belgium, who made films about reflections in puddles, three of four English including Peter Jay of the Jaywalkers, whose father ran a fairground in Lowestoft. We made what must have been one of the first music 'video' films, shot on 16mm. I liked Peter. He had a blacked out Mini Cooper with a huge tape player bolted into the dashboard and a very smart flat in Marylebone High Street, which he had painted black. Very Zen. We clustered round him as he bought us drinks and took us boating on the Thames at Henley.

There was another woman who was Australian and made films of buildings and deserted streets using tilt tripods for the Arriflex and machine noise for the sound track. She was older than most of us and had this knowing air. She was blonde, quite plain, but sexy. She lived with her husband, who was an artist and musician, on Portobello Road. Her name was Loene Serelis. One day soon after the start of the second half of the course and as I was reaching for and could just feel, the bottom, a mixture of clammy silence, its mouth sewn shut with blackened gut, she came into the Film Studios wearing a picture of a man in the form of a small brooch pinned to her left lapel.

BEYOND:

The first thing that happened when I saw His face was that I stood before a vast infinite space, unconstricted, boundless infinite space, where there was nothing. Numinous and pulsing with something beyond any love that I had ever experienced—it was for a moment a completeness of identity that included everything. Where the possibility of anything binding or confining was not just impossible, but had never been or would ever be a possibility. It was utterly without any form of negation. It was.

The next thing I remember, from this moment, without doubt the most important in my life, was the face of a man whom I instantly recognised. I then saw him as a clown, masked. Then corrected that impression and thought "Why is Loene wearing a brooch that carries a picture of my uncle?"

Then I came to. This took the time it takes for the gap between the words 'who' and 'that' in the question 'Who is that?' It took no time and yet it took *its* time…*it* was an unhurried fraction of a second that went slowly where *it* was going and took me with *it* and then returned me to where I was. But an altered me.

THE SECOND ROOM:

"Oh, you mean my badge? It's Meher Baba." I pestered her. She said she didn't really know anything about him but that she liked his face. "My husband knows all about him, you should ask him."

That evening, still crashing about trying to make sense of what had happened, I went round to their house on Portobello. The facia was an enormous swirling mural of musicians and animals and toward the centre was, once again, the face of Meher Baba in a cloud of pink roses. I knew this mural very well. I had often passed it but I had never noticed the face in the roses.

Loene's husband, Vitas, who had painted the mural, was agitatedly walking round the room in which they lived looking for a bottle opener. I asked him "Who is Meher Baba?"

He brilliantly replied, "Oh you don't want anything to do with Him. Bugger off." This was perfect and I was even more hooked. Perfect, because as I later came to know, the standard response was a lachrymose hugging and drooling of His name; if that had happened I think I would have legged it. I persevered and eventually got the address of a place in Wardour Street in Soho where I might discover more. A meeting apparently took place there each Monday evening at about six p.m. This, I now think, must have been a Friday. I can't remember the weekend.

On Monday evening I climbed up three flights of stairs, pausing to listen on each landing, until I could hear the thrum of voices. I cautiously entered feeling very nervous and slightly faint as if I was about to come face to face with Him. The small room, lit by a large arched window, was cluttered with chairs in a semi-circle facing a man in his late forties or early fifties who was carrying on badinage with a group of people standing or sitting in front of him. I slipped in and took a chair as far back as I could. Thankfully my entrance was unnoticed. The point here is that what had happened was between me and Him. I wanted no interlocutors. I wanted to find out (a) Who He was, and (b) Where He was.

The people in the room were young, though I thought not as young as I was. Long-haired men, incredibly beautiful women, all of them laughing and joking and slowly settling into their seats. I stared at the man on the chair facing us all. He had a bland but handsome face, which I could make nothing of. His hair combed neatly in a severe parting. He looked like a banker. He had a book open on his lap. He said, "Shall we be silent for a moment?" Silence fell. He was American. The atmosphere in the room deepened and I remember feeling dazed. I just stared at him. The meeting lasted for about an hour and I couldn't make sense of any of it.

I did however pick up an important fact that answered question (a): Meher Baba was God. This appeared to me to be completely appropriate and came as no surprise. In fact if He had been anything less I would have felt severely let down.

As I slipped away I touched one of the women on her arm and she turned toward me. "Where is Meher Baba?" I asked.

She answered, "He died last month, didn't you know?"

I remember the hollow echo of my steps as I returned to street level. A terrible empty banging as if cannon were going off over a vast disappearing army of humanity. Everything dwindled into a small colourless light. On the street I walked into a lamp post. When I got back to Ariel she said, "What's the blood?"

Every Monday I went back. I began to sleep. I moved into another furnished room in the next house in Oxford Gardens (ironically two doors up from Craig and Georgina San Roque and Janet Podmore, who became Ted Judson's wife, unmarried at the time; none of them I knew). I began to eat. My body was like a reed carrying this great invisible noise. My mind was a blank. In entering and leaving that place I was aware of a sort of contributory element to awareness. It's really impossible to describe. Not a heightened awareness but rather a richness, a thickening of atmosphere.

I knew nothing at that time of Baba's injunction to the West that all narcotics were spiritually harmful and should never be taken in the pursuit of any spiritual goal. In fact He had sent a kind of American legation to the West, students from Harvard, who were familiar with Laing and Kesey and Timothy Leary, and who had been briefed to spread this message of drugs' delusional effects.

The significance of this episode has always struck me as having been overlooked. In Meher Baba's physical activity, in the world during his life time, this direct focused action of His on what cannot have been more than several thousand human souls in North America and Europe stands out as being a very odd engagement. I am ignoring the declared purpose that drugs, Lysergic acid diethylamide in particular, were capable of terrible psychic destruction, and looking instead for what might be called 'the background story.' Of course it is impossible for me to say what deeper entanglements with the destiny of man Meher Baba was organizing, but the following things occur to me.

First are the three main personalities involved: Robert Dreyfuss, Alan Cohen and Rick Chapman—all three were American. Dreyfuss and Chapman had been given the opportunity to meet Baba in India. They had been told specifically to return home and spread the message that drugs were harmful, most importantly, harmful *spiritually*.

There can be no doubt that Hofmann's bicycle ride about halfway through the Second World War introduced a curious chemical to the world. He was the chemist who discovered Lysergic acid diethylamide from ergotamine in 1943. Not easily available and really only known of by professional chemists, knowledge of its results began to filter into the bohemian and artistic circles of

Europe and then in the late 1950s and early sixties to North America. It lay fallow for a while as marijuana took over the drug of choice position, but LSD and mescaline derivatives took a grip on the counter-culture when musicians began to explore music under its influence and music was its great propaganda coup.

Secondly, in Meher Baba's century, the generation that survived the Second World War were increasingly uneasy about God's ability to relieve human suffering. A secular distancing to Christianity took place in the West. This was fuelled by the disillusionment of the generation that were brought up during and just after the war, and music and art changed accordingly. Many of my generation regarded Christian society with something approaching contempt for its inability to explain human existence.

Into this vacuum, fuelled by music and populist culture, drugs emerged as a substitute. 'Getting high' is self-explanatory when regarded in this light. The 'high' offered an altered state of consciousness and LSD was the most potent of the plethora of drugs available. In fact the search for explanations for human existence and its origins are 'spiritual' by nature. The old intercessional mysticism of the established Christian churches was ending and a new alternative—ubiquitous and powerful, outside the authority of Church and State—was on offer.

That the damaging effects of LSD and indeed, all drugs were being ignored was the juncture at which Meher Baba stepped in and sent his three men from the West back to the West, armed with His love and guidance.

My own surmise (and I have no authority for this) is that Leary, a powerful, charismatic speaker, influencing with his advocacy of 'turn on, tune in and drop out' a traumatised generation, specifically in the United States, despairing at what seemed an unending war in Vietnam that was beginning to claim a lot of young American lives, was on the verge of creating a cult.

The expression of finding another way and abandoning a constricted narrow-minded bourgeoisie, was completely 'in tune' with my young generation. 'Drop out' as an injunction, from wherever it came (mostly from one's peers) made complete sense and was very inviting. Everyone knew that things had to change, and these were the things and this was the change. 'Turn on' meant using anything that took the place of this unappealing normality. LSD however provoked a serious aura of reverence and was being subsumed by Leary and others as the foundation of ritual.

Chapman, Cohen and Dreyfuss spread the word that LSD in particular and drugs in general impeded genuine spiritual search rather than enhancing it. But the side show (which I can now recognise as having Baba's tone to it) was that the meetings these three organised gathered a whole new generation of younger Americans who would never see Baba in His physical form, but would cohere into a vibrant Baba community, some of whom are now the caretakers of the spiritual centre at Myrtle Beach and contribute a core energy to the Meherabad ashram and the Meherazad abode.

Moreover, a further speculation only, is that Cohen, Dreyfuss and Chapman had been recruited by Meher Baba for a rescue mission of His Souls who were in danger of being seduced by these false prophets. Old souls that were a new generation of Baba's own, the ones that went on the 1969 *Darshan*, and as I have said, the ones that subsequently became the caretakers of Myrtle Beach. They formed a core to work with the mandali until they dropped their bodies, and then along with others in India and Europe, would become the next generation of caretakers at Meherabad and Meherazad.

The meetings continued. The film course ended. My allowance came to an end with my father telling me that now was the time to get a trade. I had a trade. It was called Love. I don't think I actually ever said that to him; there would have been a problem. But things were happening. I met a girl at a party given by a former girlfriend of mine. She took me in, this stringy waif. Her place was civilised, comfortable, organised, warm and entertaining. Angela brought me back to life, but inside me was this determination to get to India where Meher Baba had his ashram.

*****

William now lives with his wife, cultivating his garden in the mountains of the South of France.

101 Tales of Finding Love

YOUR LOVING GRACE

by Susie Biddu

Real Happiness
Lies in Making Others Happy
Avatar Meher Baba

Image © Meher Nazar Publications

Susie Biddu

My first taste of India was looking up from my receptionist's desk whilst working at NEMS Enterprises, in London and seeing four young men, dressed from top to bottom in spotless white pajamas with garlands of sandalwood beads around their necks. They were the biggest musical sensation in the world, John, Paul, George and Ringo. Little did I know that a few years later, I would constantly sleep in those same white cotton pajamas, and that at the very same time the Beatles had crossed from England to India to be with the Maharishi, my unknown future husband (Biddu) had crossed from India to England. While the BBC was interviewing him as India's #1 pop star, the Beatles were meditating with the Maharishi.

Let's start at the beginning: I had a lovely upbringing in London—really nice parents, working-class, good people. I grew up feeling I was the richest girl in the neighborhood. When I look back, we were probably the poorest. They made a wonderful loving home for me and my three brothers. My father was very principled—if we couldn't pay for it we didn't have it. As I grew up, I always wanted to be helpful and I hated to see anyone suffer. I loved dancing and singing. Mum took my brother, Richard, and me to the local Church hall for singing and dance classes. We performed on stage at a very early age.

I had a slight Christian upbringing—we went to the local Sunday school and I was attracted to Christ and wanted always to please Him—I was very afraid of hell. I didn't like the idea of being sent there to stoke the flames. It occurred to me even as a small child, why would a God be so merciless to all those people of different colour and religions, who couldn't read the Bible or understand English. It was hardly their fault if they were born into a womb in a different part of the world.

I always felt there was a Presence watching me. I behaved properly—I didn't want to disappoint my family. I rebelled in other ways: tons of make-up, up-to-date clothes, a severe need of freedom, and I hated being told what to do. I was always conscious of people's suffering and as a little girl often wished for a magic wand to make people's hurt go away. But like all little girls, I had to grow up.

When I was a teenager, unlike any of my friends, I was fascinated by Eastern Mysticism and would read books by authors like Lobsang Rampa. It felt quite normal to me to have astral experiences. Lamas living in caves, meditating and having out-of-body experiences all seemed quite natural. I never had a problem with reincarnation, it all fitted into place. The Happy Hippy era was truly alive in London in my late teens. The music was fantastic, the youth had never been so free and there was plenty of work when you wanted it.

I wasn't very academic and left school really early, much to my parents' disappointment. Because I could do a bit of modeling, promotion work and acting, I would work a few months, just to raise enough money so I could travel. I never really had thoughts of marriage, settling down, owning anything.

I had been traveling for almost a year throughout Spain and thought that I should go back to England and see my parents. This was September 1969. I had met a girlfriend in Spain and she said, "If you ever come to London, please stay with us." So I arrived quite unexpectedly at 39 Russell Road, West London. The significance of this address will come later. This lovely girl, Cathy, opened the door to me, and we just clicked!

I said, "There's a club round the corner called Blazes, why don't we go there?" I was dressed in all my Biba clothes (a very fashionable boutique at that time), two pairs of false eyelashes, six-inch platform shoes, extra hairpiece, black lips and nails—thinking I was the cat's whiskers! Arriving at the club, I looked down the stairs and there was this apparition: a tall, slim young man with long black hair down to his shoulders, a gold band round his head, dressed in a suede shirt and trousers, with long tassels attached, bare-chested with a large crucifix around his neck.

Susie Biddu

He looked up at me and said, in a very deep American accent, "Do you girls want me to sign you in?" This mysterious, dark-skinned Apache-looking young man later asked me to dance. When the club closed he offered us a lift home. I thought, "Why not?"

I suggested that he come in for a cup of tea at my friend's flat in Russell Road. When he entered the lounge, he picked up a guitar in the corner and started strumming and singing, as I put the kettle on. I, who had worked for the Beatles and had been in the music industry, thought, "Wow, he's got talent!" He sang a couple of songs that he had written. He had a fabulous voice. Whilst leaving, he asked if I would see him again and give him my number. I took his.

I gave him a call three days later. He came round and by the end of the evening, I knew he was from East India. His father had been a doctor and died seven years earlier. He had been a very successful singer in India, possibly India's first pop star. He had ambitions to make it in the West, and for the past two years in London, he had been making donuts at the American Embassy to fund producing and writing songs for records. I had never met anyone like him.

I got a job in England, and supported myself while he strummed his guitar all night, hoping to come up with the next big hit record. He concentrated on song writing and producing. I felt a fascination for his Eastern background. I had never met anyone so confident in himself, talented, understated and not materialistic—a heady combination. He was refreshing. I was rather frustrated by his complete lack of money and often missed going out to restaurants, clubs and having a more fun time. But there was never a doubt in him that he would make it.

Four months after we met, his friend, Suresh, who was studying at Boston University called and said he had an American friend who wanted to make a record. The only person Suresh knew was Biddu in London. They arranged a ticket for him to fly to New

41

York, leaving me behind! I decided to give in my notice at work and arranged for us to meet up in America a few weeks later. We spent three wonderful months there, with the parents of Mark Etra, whom Biddu was producing. Finally the record was made and Biddu and I had to return to London. We had had a taste of luxury in America.

On our return we rented a flat in Earls Court, near where I was born. He was still writing songs and he didn't have a job, but had managed to save some of the fee Mark had paid him for the record, just enough to buy a ticket to India. He hadn't been home to India or seen his mother for years. There, he saw an astrologer. He sent me a telegram saying, "Will you marry me?" The astrologer had told him to marry me, so we got married on June 2 in England, in the same church I had been christened in. I had asked Biddu to please arrange a vintage car to take me to the church, a distance of about one hundred yards—the one luxury I wanted. When it arrived for the two-minute journey, it turned out to be King George V's Daimler. The emblem on the bonnet was the Indian *Natraj*! This car had been to India.

Biddu signed up Carl Douglas (who sang the song "Kung Fu Fighting"), Tina Charles, and Jimmy James, financing their records, then selling the product to the record companies, so he always owned the product. Finally, we had enough money to buy ourselves tickets to India. I could meet my in-laws for the first time. We had been together for six years, and I still hadn't met a member of his family! Now he was taking home his British bride. Who felt more Indian than he did!

I was still reading a lot of mystical books, still going to church, doing some charity work, seeing clairvoyants—my reading material for India, was *Siddhartha* by Herman Hesse. We left London for India in December—Biddu, the prodigal son, returning to his hometown Bangalore. First to Bombay, to meet all his friends, then to Bangalore to meet all the in-laws, then to Rajasthan to ride on elephants!

Susie Biddu

As I got off the plane in Bombay, I felt so at home, everything so familiar. I just loved the smells, the colour, the people, oh yes, the people, the smiles, the friendliness. The only thing that made me so angry was the fact that his friends lived in these apartment blocks, while on the pavement outside lived the very poor in squalid conditions—little children dressed in rags with no shoes on their feet, living worse than animals. I was appalled and could hardly sleep. I felt so guilty. Their plight and poverty were ignored by the locals, as though they didn't exist. It was shocking and I felt great disdain for the people around me.

The first night in Bombay, in Suresh's apartment in Colaba, I thought, "Something's happened here." I couldn't put my finger on it.

I loved my in-laws—they were very sweet and delightful. We had to meet a tremendous number of people whilst in Bangalore. It was ten days of constant talking and eating. Everybody was interesting and friendly. One unusually quiet afternoon in Biddu's mother's garden, I had just finished the book *Siddhartha* when a butterfly landed on my hand. I felt a tremendous peace, contentment, an opening up of consciousness. A feeling of Oneness. Another day Biddu's uncle asked me if I wanted to go to Whitefield, where a guru called Satya Sai Baba had an ashram. I had never been to an ashram and had never heard of this person, so rather curious, I said yes. Apparently his uncle was one of the closest disciples of Satya Sai Baba. He was a small man dressed in a long orange robe with masses of dark frizzy hair, singing on the stage. I was really excited by the whole charged atmosphere. Here was devotion. It was far removed from my everyday life in the West. I felt a longing, a home-sickness for the life of a devotee.

Before getting on the plane to return home, I got on my knees on the tarmac of the airport and kissed the ground. I really, really wanted to return again and again to Mother India. On the plane going home, there was a sadhu in light-coloured saffron robes. I felt attracted to him as I sat next to him, he handed me a small photo of a man with a headband sitting on a wall. It was a photo of Sai Baba of Shirdi. I was captivated and kept that small photo with me for years.

What I was not prepared for on our return to London was that I didn't know what was happening to me. It was utterly terrifying. I lost all joy and reason to live. Everything became meaningless. I just knew, without any doubt that I had lived so many times before and it was all useless, all a dream, a continuous endless dream with no value. In my head, I kept saying "Why? You promised me that I wouldn't have to do this again. You promised that I wouldn't have to return and here I am, doing it all over again. God, You broke Your promise. I've done this one hundred thousand times before, and You promised me I didn't have to do this again." I had no idea where this was all coming from.

But I knew with certainty that life was pointless, that everything that I would achieve, every success I would have, everything I acquired— homes, cars, fame, even those whom I loved I would have to say goodbye to. So why don't I kill myself now? What is the point of delaying the inevitable? Even now, all these years later, I am afraid of those thoughts. At the time, I had no understanding, no one to talk to, as I didn't have the language to articulate what was happening to me. The crazy thing was that I had always been a happy and positive person. It was so out of character. Meanwhile Biddu was having this wonderful success, and I couldn't be less interested. I had no use for the world. I did not want to be in it. But I knew I couldn't kill myself, some deep Christian belief that suicide was frowned upon stopped me.

We had been invited to France late in January, to Midem, a music festival held every year in Cannes, where Biddu was to be given a big award. Everyone there congratulated us, whilst I was thinking, "It's all nonsense, nothing is real." Frightened, I didn't leave the hotel room, didn't even go to the Award ceremony.

I thought, "When I go back to London, I will have to tell Biddu I need to go back to India and live in one of those ashram places." I would feel safe there. I could contemplate a relationship with

God, live a simple life. That way I knew I could survive. Looking back after years, I realize now that Baba had pulled back the veil for a few weeks. Not knowing of Baba and His teachings at that time, I was lost. Biddu had no clue of what was happening to me. I didn't know myself, so how could I explain it to someone else. I seriously thought I was going mad.

When we got back to London I had become physically ill. I went to the doctors and took the tests in the morning and received a call from the doctor's surgery in the afternoon, with the astonishing news that I was pregnant! My mind flew back to the first night in India in Suresh's apartment in Bombay. That was the feeling I had, that something had happened. Well, it sure had. I couldn't kill myself now, no going off to an ashram or convent for me, no turning my back on this world. I would have to find the one and only thing worth living for —ETERNAL LOVE— whilst living in the middle of Illusion.

I started coming back to normality, because of this baby business. I began to write to nuns, to orphanages, do voluntary work. I felt I had to be useful. We now had a big house I was doing up, having a baby, coping with Biddu's great success. I took up Transcendental Meditation, religiously meditated morning and night during my pregnancy, read about different religions, felt drawn to Hinduism, visited different sects and religious groups, spent time in church, searching for meaning.

My conscious mind returned full force to materialism. Enjoying success, loving my baby boy and being a mother, having money and being able to be generous with our families and friends. My spiritual search still continued and we went back to India often, taking our baby boy with us to visit our Indian family and friends. Then in 1977, a friend and I took our two small boys to Spain on holiday. Sitting at the port in Marbella, this attractive Dutch boy, Robert Bloeme, came up to me. He said, "I hear you have a home here. Would you like to buy a painting?"

"Yes."

"I also hear that you go to India often. Have you heard of Meher Baba?"

I looked him in the eye and said, "I am so Baba'd out, please don't come back and give me anything!"

The next night, he came back with a Baba book. It was Phyllis Frederick's *The Path of Love*. Being a polite person, I took it.

I went home and read it all night from cover to cover. From that moment to now, I have never doubted Meher Baba's divinity. I went straight back to London and met everybody who had ever met Him: Hilde Halpern, Dorothy and Tom Hopkinson, Fred Marks, Delia DeLeon and Don Stevens. I got completely and utterly involved with the Meher Baba Association. Pete Townshend was just closing down Oceanic. We had our meetings in the Quaker centre near Leicester Square. Then we had the opportunity of purchasing from Maxine Summers the basement flat underneath Don Stevens flat in Hammersmith Grove.

I immediately organized events for us all to be together. One Saturday afternoon we took a boat trip from Richmond to Kew Gardens, where Baba had visited, decorating the boat with pink balloons and hearts. It was such a lovely day that I decided to take my mother on the same boat trip the next day. As we went past the Petersham Hotel, where Baba had visited in 1931, my mother said, "Sue, I've got a picture of you when you were three years old, right there." It was under the balcony that Baba had stood with Delia, in the 1930s!

The moment that I heard about Baba, I read as many books about His life as possible. I watched all the films available, attended Delia's meetings every week. It was thrilling. He so often moved me to tears. Every question I had in my head He would answer. Once after the closing of Oceanic, I came back from the event completely saturated with His Love. I had an out-of-body experience for a couple of days—floating around with no substance. I realized that this was a very delightful but dangerous state of mind. After that, there have been very few of those experiences—they don't seem necessary or practical anymore.

It came to me whilst reading that Baba had stayed at Kitty Davy's home in Russell Road, the same road that I had stayed in when I first met Biddu. I was at number 39—Baba stayed at number 32. This was the first house He stayed in on His first visit to the West, in 1931, seventy years to the day of the Twin Towers. I remember being at Meherazad that winter after Eruch had passed away, hearing the story of Eruch and Baba leaving New York for the last time in 1958. Baba asked Eruch to turn around, and in hand gestures said, "It will fall in, like a pack of cards."

We went to Myrtle Beach where I wanted to meet Kitty and Margaret. We took Zak, our son, with us. It was my first visit, and I'm a very poor sleeper. We had a cabin for the three of us, and all night I was restless, disturbing Biddu and Zak.

First thing in the morning, I called Kitty. I said, "Hi Kitty I'm Susie Biddu, and I'm from London. I know St. Paul's girls' school where you were a pupil, and I met my Indian husband when I was living at 39 Russell Road. I know that Baba stayed in your family home at 32 Russell Road, where he gathered His early English lovers, returning twice afterwards."

She said, "But my dear, I was born at #39, and the family only moved to #32 when it got bigger!"

I said, "Can you help me? I'm having problems sleeping and that's disturbing my young child and husband in our room."

She said, "Why don't you go and spend the nights in the Lagoon Cabin?"
So, on my first visit to Myrtle Beach I spent all nine nights in the Lagoon Cabin! With permission! I used to stare at His chair for hours on end, weeping throughout the night. I was definitely in the honeymoon stage. I met so many wonderful people: Kitty, Jane Haynes, Darwin Shaw, Margret Craske, Wendy Haynes, Jane

and Bob Brown. I visited Myrtle Beach often, loving Baba's bedroom in the home that Elizabeth had built so lovingly for Him. We have just refurbished the London Centre, in Hammersmith Grove. The upstairs room, where Don once lived, houses Baba's Pink Coat, given to Pete Townshend by Mani. The atmosphere is similar.

I had a strong wish to go to Meherazad, where Baba had lived. I have no memory of my first visit to the Samadhi. But over the years I have been fortunate to visit this timeless place hundreds if not thousands of times. It is the only place that has never changed for me in this ever-changing world. It is the place where, when I kneel and put my head on the marble slab that says "I have not come to teach but to awaken," I truly feel myself, no hidden corners, no kidding. He knows Me and He loves me. Nothing else matters. I had come Home, after such a long time. (As I write this, I am crying.) His care and compassion for me have been beyond words.

*****

I became Chairman of the Association, worked as a consultant in a property company and returned to being a volunteer at The Royal Brompton Hospital, which specializes in the treatment of heart, lungs and cancers. During this time both my parents and brother were diagnosed with cancer. We see such a small part of the picture of our existence. It's like a jigsaw puzzle, seeing only a few pieces, we don't see the whole picture. It's there but we only see what is in front of us, not seeing the past, present and future until the puzzle is completed. My family's illness and deaths were made bearable by Baba's Grace.

Now, I am most fortunate to be able to spend three to five months in India every year. My longstanding and patient husband sits at the Retreat dining room, declaring himself an atheist. He, who has probably visited Meherabad more than most Baba lovers! And every year, my respect for the residents increases—what a life they have lived and what service they have given. This is the first time that I have written my story, so thank you to the editor for asking. Finally, thank You, Baba, for making it possible for me to find You and Your mandali this lifetime, and enabling me to live in the loving atmosphere of Meherabad. Meeting Your new and old lovers, hearing the fantastic stories of how Your love and grace called them. For this and so much else, I am truly thankful.

101 Tales of Finding Love

FINDING GOD AS A CHILD

by Debby Blackman

Godman enters his own creation to tend us, His flowers

1984

MEHER BABA AUSTRALIA

Artwork © Claire Mataira

*"Childhood is the ideal period of life in which to take an interest in spiri-
tuality. The impressions received at a young age become deeply ingrained."*
—Meher Baba, Lord Meher, pg. 982

When I was a child, Jesus became a living, breathing person
to me. He was much more than a character in a story;
His life was the model for who I wanted to become. I loved His
gentle ways, the love He expressed for every living creature, the
forgiveness He showed to those who made mistakes, and the par-
ables He told. This love did not stem from going to church and
was not taught to me by my parents; God just seemed to find me
and I Him.

I don't remember how Jesus and I met. My family was not religious even though my mother's father was a Methodist minister.
My first memory of my relationship with Jesus was when I was
four or five, and it was through a book that I found among my
sister's things, *Bible Stories for Young People* by Lillie A. Faris. I
loved that book. It had beautiful illustrations that were photos of
oil or watercolor paintings and printed onto that especially fine
heavyweight, glossy paper that was used in expensive books. One
of my favorite illustrations was of Jesus with a staff in His hand,
herding a flock of sheep. This was a simple black and white
sketch found on the inside covers and facing pages of the book. I
would trace this picture onto a piece of typing paper and color it,
repeating the process many times. I believed the stories in this
book: that God saved Daniel in the lions' den and Moses from
the rushes, that Jesus loved me and that He was God incarnate.

It is interesting that my sister also grew up loving Jesus. Maybe
she was my first conduit to the Beloved. She has no memory of
religious instruction but her love for Jesus continues to guide her
life as a Mormon. My love for Jesus led me to Meher Baba. Our

mutual love for God is the hand in which our sisterhood resides and I thank Baba for making it so.

How to be more Christ-like? That was what I wanted more than anything. There was no one to talk to about this and not any guidance or satisfaction in the instruction I got when attending church camp with friends or by sitting in Sunday School on a very irregular basis. I would notice behavior and characteristics in others that seemed to match my idea of what was "good," but it was not always easy to emulate. What seemed to be instinctual for them was not for me—with my serious disposition and extreme self-consciousness as a child. I did not yet understand that Jesus was within me not just outside of me.

There were no guide books for children or adolescents on how to find a deeper path to God. My parents raised me to be polite, kind, independent and truthful. They encouraged me to always do my best and taught me to be true to myself. These lessons were always helpful but I knew there were deeper truths to be known as well.

It appeared I had to work my way to what I sought, just like most of us have to, but with no idea how to do this. Throughout adolescence I experienced depression, isolation, shame and self-consciousness, with no sense of who I really was. At the age of twenty-four I came in contact with Michael Hughes through a teaching friend of mine. He led me through a type of self-inventory of my life and the family dynamics and events that influenced my thoughts and feelings. Afterwards, Michael encouraged me to come teach at a boy's group home, and participate in a staff-training center that was based on Buddhist teachings. From there I started practicing *Nyingma* Buddhism and learned through its practices to clearly look at the emotions and fears that had me tethered to a very uncomfortable and dissatisfying place. In the early 1980s, the American culture was learning to express its feelings, while I, who already tended to be controlled by emotions, was learning to keep mine on a tighter leash.

Baba entered my life through Ken Blackman, a man who would be my husband, friend and support on our souls' journeys. He first provided me with reading materials which frightened me. Unable to imagine that I would ever have the strength or desire to lead the life of one of Meher Baba's followers, I wasn't interested in giving myself to a Master. It was too foreign of an idea, and the thought of letting go of my will and giving in to another's was very scary. How to give myself up to a Master when it seemed I had nothing to give? How to become the dust at Baba's feet when I already felt like dust blowing in every direction? I didn't feel solid enough to be broken apart. Not yet. Then in one book Baba indicated that a disciple had to be a rock in order to become the dust, and that was an idea to which I could relate; it corresponded to what I intuited for myself.

I stuck with my Buddhist practices, dealt with my hypoglycemia, and eventually took anti-depressants. Read more about Baba and participated in Baba groups in Seattle and Tucson. I did not refer to myself as a Baba lover for a long time. I appreciated Baba's teachings but was not able to accept him as God—this might mean I would have to let go of my beloved Jesus. However, over the course of decades Jesus and Baba morphed into one. The fact that the photos of Baba in His younger years are similar to the pictures of Jesus at the same age made the transfer of love easier. Baba said that He and Jesus were one and the same. Not just that, but that He was Buddha as well, and Ram and Krishna and all the Avatars. I never liked the Christian idea that only Christians would go to heaven—God loved everyone, and all who loved Him would be with Him always. Dear Baba kept drawing me closer.

I began to experience Baba in ways that were unique to me. He seemed to appear everywhere. For example, at my women's retreats, Baba would be there dressed in costumes and dancing with us, always smiling. He would show up in the conga line at the Los Angeles sahavas. He would be at my shoulder as I was in my classroom teaching, constantly reminding me that these were His children with whom I was interacting. He actually seemed to be at my side guiding me and laughing with me and at me. His poster-sized picture hung in my classroom, reminding students and teacher alike to "DON'T WORRY, BE HAPPY."

Dreams of Baba brought me joy. He allowed me to experience sincere appreciation for my parents and the safety and love He had provided for me. He even seemed to perform a few tiny "miracles" that in a very clear way helped me to understand how to perform the service He had given me. It felt as though I was simply a worker ant and I felt a desperate need to do what He wanted me to do.

When I became ill in 2003 with chronic lyme disease, He encouraged me to depend more and more on Him. He taught me lessons in patience, strength, and faith. I learned to be cheerful despite my having to give up teaching, my social life, my energy, and independence. Giving up teaching was the hardest because that was how I could provide service to Him. I went into despair wondering how to be of any service to anyone, even my family. My life was turned topsy-turvy in what turned out to be one of the greatest blessings of my life. I spent many hours with Baba, talking to Him, constantly repeating "I am helpless and hopeless." I memorized the Parvadigar Prayer and the Prayer of Repentance, turned to Him for comfort and felt His love. When I was extremely ill He showed me that pain and death were not as frightening as I had once thought. It was during this time that I knew I was truly His. My illness was and continues to be a blessing in that through it I learn to love Baba more deeply than ever seemed possible. When I remember to, I feel Him within me now, down to my bones.

On Amartithi, January 31, 2017, Ken and I had lunch with other Baba lovers and then went to sit and eat dessert in one our favorite places, the Champaign Book Store. As we were talking I was scanning the book shelves and a book-binding jumped out at me. There on the shelf was a copy of *Bible Stories for Young People*, my conduit to Jesus and then to Baba. I walked over, took it from the shelf, and through tears of delight and astonishment, once again, leafed my way through the illustrations. What a truly marvelous Amartithi gift from Baba!

*****

Debby lives in Asheville, North Carolina, with her husband, son, and an assortment of dogs.

101 Tales of Finding Love

A New Lease on Life

by Ken Blackman

At Mandali Hall, Meherazad, 1998. Left to right: Saunder Blackman, Dolly Dastur, Steven Blackman, Bal Natu, Ken Blackman.

In considering how to share something so important in my life
as my relationship with Meher Baba, it seems at once so simple and yet so impossible. I guess if this seems paradoxical and
'mysterious' then that would certainly convey a significant 'flavor'
of my journey with Baba. It was somewhere around 1998, twenty-
five years after first learning about Meher Baba, that I first traveled to Meherabad, India, where Baba's body resides (His *Samadhi*). My two sons, Steven, eight, and Saunder, fourteen, were
along 'for the ride.' The fact that I had two sons, and, for that
matter, the fact that I was still alive at all, I attributed to the reality that Meher Baba had somehow seen it fitting to enter into my
life. Growing up shy and 'sensitive,' with my dad distant and often away and my mom coping in part with alcohol, I longed for
something 'different.' For some souls, depression, confusion and
despair can often accompany such circumstances. My 'different'
contained many distractions with drugs, alcohol, women, etc. But
I also sought answers through psychology and spirituality.

I recall well, upon visiting Meherazad on that trip to India, meeting some of Baba's mandali (close followers) and being deeply
'jolted' upon seeing the 'magical and renowned' Blue Bus in which
Baba and many of His disciples had travelled around India.
'Jolted,' because it suddenly dawned on me how mischievous and
incredibly thoughtful and sweet Baba had been with me. For in
my journey I now realized that Baba had been with me over the
years in ways I had never understood or fathomed.

I had spent much of my adolescence traveling regularly from New
Jersey to New York City, mainly to find ways to get drunk—it
wasn't particularly hard to find ways in NYC. In 1972 I was back
in NYC, with my degree in Psychology, attending Arica Spiritual
programs and trying to find ways to get enlightened. It was here
that I met Michael, who introduced me to the teachings and life
story of Meher Baba. The books I was given to read covered
many topics I had seriously pondered throughout my life, and the

depth and authority of Baba's words moved me deeply. I was however, to be sure, still depressed and confused. I continued to read and absorb as much as I could from various Baba books and headed off to Boston to participate in a forty-day spiritual intensive Arica program, hoping desperately for some kind of relief and inner awakening.

No doubt the training helped me in many ways, but at the end I was still teetering on hopelessness and futility. As powerful as Baba's words were, He had passed in 1969 and I thought I needed a living 'teacher' to guide and support me. And so it came as a surprise when I was told that the altar I had created and used throughout the forty days had mysteriously burned down, destroying everything on it but leaving, unscathed, a picture of Baba with the words "Don't worry Be Happy" (something I wished were possible). I could find no rational manner to explain away the nature of fire choosing such a selective display of burning things to a crisp, and surrendered to the possibility I was receiving a message of some sort. I was spontaneously and sincerely moved to declare, to this no longer living 'Baba,' that if He could somehow help me I would repay Him by dedicating my life to helping others as best I could.

Certainly there was no instant miraculous huge change in my inner state but I did now have some sense of possibility of hope. And so I kept breathing and moved on to Philadelphia to participate as a trainer in the Arica programs. One helpful thing I had realized through these trainings was that disillusionment and suicidal depression might possibly be a part of the ascending spiritual trajectory towards awakening to a truth that transcends the limited ego. Not much comfort, but some.

I decided now to make a journey down to the Meher Spiritual Center in Myrtle Beach, again desperately hoping for something/someone to help me. I did get there and someone did help me and recalling how I was 'jolted' in India now comes into play. That I only realized the connection I am about to share after more than twenty years, I still find astounding. I had little money and no vehicle and despite extensive searching could not find something fitting to travel in. One day, out of the blue, someone showed up at my doorstep with a 1968 Dodge long bed van with windows all around; perfect in every way to make into a camper. For me. For seven hundred bucks. Which I could afford. Too good to be true. Did I mention it was blue. It was in this blue bus that I then travelled to the Meher Center and it was in this blue bus that, it so happened, someone did come to me and did help me in ways I never could have imagined possible. And it was as I stood staring at a similar blue bus at Meherazad, India so many years later, that I realized Baba had manifested this ' replica' of His blue bus for me to travel to meet Him on the ocean shores of Myrtle Beach.

I arrived at the Meher Center in pretty much the same state of mind I had spent much of my life trying to ignore or avoid—lost, unlovable, worthless, scared. I was really nervous about going somewhere where others might be happy, spiritually advanced, way above my pitiful self. (No one else really knew this hidden aspect of my inner life.) Two friends and I arrived at the center gateway and were told they were not yet open and we were directed to a beach park close by to bide our time.

I parked the Blue Bus looking out at the vast ocean and drifted off into an 'altered state' in which something rather profound and magical happened. I found myself standing outside of the Center boundary, terrified to 'cross over.' Then I saw someone walking towards me (more like floating, really), cross the Center boundary and approach me directly. Long flowing hair, white sadra, magical loving eyes. "Must be Baba. I gotta get outta here before I'm exposed in all my awfulness."

But His eyes hold me fast, and I begin to show Him all the reasons no one should/could love me; and He just showers me with understanding, compassion, and pure acceptance. So I show him more bad stuff and He intensifies His showering of complete love and acceptance. Oh boy, this is something I am not prepared for and have no frame of reference with which to comprehend. But I cannot deny the raw truth of His intensity and convic-

tion; He obviously is not buying my story and clearly has His own agenda. He then (really) picks me up and throws me up high in the air and I come down in His arms and am younger. This continues several times until I finally return to His arms as an infant, hopeless and helpless, yet totally safe in His embrace. A difficult position to argue from. But I worry that somehow I do not deserve this and others should really be its recipient. His response is clear and unmistakable. He casts His glance out on the entire creation (truly) and conveys with NO doubt that this Love He is showering on me is there for all of creation. I immediately and spontaneously recognize this as 'Divine Love.'

All this took place as I lay in this Blue Bus He had sent to bring me Home.

This encounter has served as my touchstone these last forty-some years as I continue to wend my way 'home' for good. As I recall this now, gratitude and awe resonate within my heart for the gifts Meher Baba has, and continues to bestow upon me. And if He finds me worthy, then it must be so, as He is the most loving Friend, Teacher, Master and Companion I could have ever wished for. Jai Baba.

*****

Ken is semi-retired from his private practice of Naturopathic Medicine and Psychotherapy and now lives in Asheville, North Carolina with wife Debby. He realized his dream of building his own house and now looks forward to more hiking, kayaking and general outdoor activities. He is also a Board Member of the Meher Archive Collective, working to identify, preserve and make available to the world all materials related to Baba's life.

101 Tales
of Finding Love

MY PERSONAL JOURNEY
TO AVATAR MEHER BABA

by Cyrus Bomanji

Artwork © Claire Mataira

Cyrus Bomanji

MY FIRST MEETING WITH A PERFECT MASTER:

As a child I had rectal prolapse when very young (around six or seven years old). I had an operation but it was not successful, so my parents started going to the Sai Baba temple in Bombay to seek his blessings. After my second operation, which was successful, we started following Sai Baba. We visited Shirdi and also started attending *aarti* (prayers) every Thursday at a Sai Baba shrine near our home in Bombay. A few years later I suddenly awoke from my sleep one night and saw Sai Baba standing right in front of me and blessing me. I tried to wake my mother up but she was fast asleep. I felt so happy and blessed to see that miraculous sight. It lasted only a few moments, and I did not understand its significance and importance at that young an age. This was my first meeting with a Perfect Master.

As years passed by, we stopped going to the local Sai Baba temple and my father started following his own religious beliefs, but it did not stop our family visiting other saints/masters such as Ajmer Sharif and Maulana Saheb, to name a couple, to seek their blessings. But none of these did we follow as disciples.

INTRODUCTION TO MEHER BABA:

I cannot recollect exactly when I heard the name Meher Baba, however I got to hear of Him through my mother. My mother had told me, "There is someone called Meher Baba and He is God, just like Sai Baba". I did not ask any further questions or show any more interest. I would be given sweets by my mother when she visited the Bombay Meher Baba Centre and I would accept the *prasad*. Though I respected Meher Baba, I somehow did not have any curiosity to know Him whatsoever. As time passed by, I started showing some interest in going to the Bombay Centre and slowly I started to be drawn in and I felt I liked going there.

I have come across the message that no one comes to Him unless He wants this to happen and I believe this to be true. To illustrate it, I would like to share a short story concerning my parents. They filed their income tax returns for twenty-five years next to the Meher Baba Bombay Centre but not once did they enquire what the Centre was about or whose picture was hanging on the door to the Centre, etc. It is indeed strange that for twenty-five years Baba was right next to us, but we had not 'found' Him yet, as our time had not come for Him to enter into our lives.

FIRST EXPERIENCE OF MEHER BABA BEING OMNIPRESENT:

After my college graduation I was working for a consulate in Bombay, but left my job as I could not cope with the Consul General's hot temper. I went through a short phase when I could not find a job, although I was constantly searching for one. It was felt by the recruiting agents or recruiters that I would not last long in the jobs that were being offered to me.

One day the doorbell rang; it was an old man in a turban (a *Sikh*) asking for a donation to his cause. I told him that I did not have any money, but if I did get a job I would make a donation. The old man wished me good luck and gave me a picture of Guru Nanakji, (the Sikh Perfect Master). He told me that when I did get a job I should visit a Guru Nanak temple and place some donation at His *Dargah*. I agreed, and the *Sardarji* left.

During the same period, I had applied for a job in the airline industry and I got selected. But on completion of the airline's medicals, the doctor diagnosed that I had 'two heart beats,' i.e. a heart murmur, and if that was confirmed on further examination, I would not be offered the job.

I was very scared on hearing this news, however my mother had told me that when I was in difficulty I should keep repeating Meher Baba's name. So when I was going through the medicals again, I was continuously taking His Name, and consoled myself by saying that even if I had two heartbeats, Meher Baba would make

68

sure my 'murmur' was not detected! I am not sure why, but I had that conviction because of what my mother had said to me and I believed it one hundred percent.

The medical tests were done and there was no heart murmur detected. However, I did not get the job! All my other friends who had applied for the same role had been accepted. I was the only one who had not been selected after the medicals! It was a very good job offer and I would have liked to be part of that organisation, but obviously Meher Baba had other plans lined up for me!

After few days I was feeling restless again as I still did not have employment; so out of sheer frustration I looked at Meher Baba's picture at home, in front of which we stood before for our prayers. I said to Him, almost challenged Him, "You, Meher Baba, say you are GOD. Tell me then, when will I find a job?" But a voice within me seemed to say, "Why are you asking Me when will you get a job? Ask me instead WHEN you want a job?!"

I was a little taken aback with the turn in this conversation with Meher Baba, to say the least! I blurted out to this inner voice, "27th then," little realising as I then looked at the calendar, that the date was too distant, wishing instead that I had said an earlier date. But now the die was cast, and I would be spending more days of restlessness till the 27th arrived. (I might add that I did not take this inner conversation seriously, and dismissed it as my mind's own imagination.)

I shall NEVER forget receiving a call on the afternoon of 26th May, 2000 from the company to which I had applied for a job, telling me that I had been selected and I was to come the very next day to sign the employment contracts accepting the offer of employment. I was in total ecstasy and so happy and overjoyed. I was over the moon at this turn of events! I gave the good news to my parents and then went and stood before Meher Baba's picture saying THANK YOU, THANK YOU, THANK YOU!

That afternoon as I lay down in bed, my eyes wandered over to the calendar hanging on the wall and I was totally shaken to see that it was indeed 27th May tomorrow, when I would be going to sign my employment contract for the new job! I was shocked and dumbfounded by this whole experience.

This then was my first experience of Meher Baba's Omnipresence.

Leaving all to Baba's Will—the working of His will in my life:

After I joined the company in May 2000, I met a friend who had been part of a batch of recruits selected before me, and who was going to Zurich through the company.

I, in an instant, said to Baba, "Baba, if you want me to go to Zurich, I will go to Zurich." I cannot fathom for a moment what had come over me to make me say that to Baba.

However, just a few months after joining the company, my manager called me and two other work colleagues over. He told us that we would all be flying to Zurich in November for a week so we should be sorting out our passports and keep them ready.

I had already applied for my passport, so again I said to Baba that only if you want me to go to Zurich will I want to go. The passport process in India in those days took a long time and it was very likely and possible that it would not be ready by November. But, once again, Baba worked His magic and my passport was issued on 31st October. It arrived a week later, on Thursday, and was duly submitted the same day for a Swiss visa, which I got the next day. I flew out to Zurich the following week.

All these experiences I have recounted above have brought me closer to Beloved Baba. Looking at Baba's picture, I can only smile and be grateful for His benevolence and for keeping His *nazar* on me.

Cyrus Bomanji

He was also Zoroaster:

I still remember the day I was travelling with my dad on a Mumbai bus, No. 220, near Bandra station, a suburb of Bombay, and my father told me that Baba was Zoroaster. I got annoyed when he said this, and asked him to please stop misusing or misrepresenting Baba's words, as I had not come across any message from Baba declaring that He was Zoroaster. I had only ever read that Baba was Rama, Krishna and Buddha.

When I reached home and was randomly leafing through a Meher Baba book, I read a quote of Baba's which said that He was Zoroaster. Again I was surprised and taken aback to read those words of Baba's. It was as though Meher Baba had been listening to me arguing with my father. I had to abjectly apologise to my father for my ignorance.

My immediate thought was, "How fascinating to think of the attention that Meher Baba seemed to give to my 'rantings' and to provide the answers to me in His own way!" As someone had correctly said to me, Meher Baba is a personal God. He is always standing by our side, right next to us, but we cannot see Him physically present because we are blinded by *maya* and enveloped by our earthly weaknesses of lust, anger and greed.

Baba's Will vs my Will:

Baba lovers always face a dilemma to understand whether it is their will or God's will working in their lives.

I faced the same problem. One day when travelling to Meherazad, a random thought cropped up in my head, "Baba has always said not a leaf moves without His will, nor do waves roll without His will." Me being me, I took this further and thought to myself, "If that is the case, then if I do bad or hurt someone it is because of Baba's will. So all my bad actions are part of His will and not mine." I was contemplating these thoughts, but when I reached Meherazad I forgot all about them.

71

We saw Baba's movie in the Mandali hall, and after the movie was over I got up to leave. Right there in front of me was a message displayed with the following words: "Think thoughts you would not hesitate to think in My presence. Speak words you would not hesitate to speak in My presence. And do things you would not hesitate to do in My presence."

I had the answer to my random thought—to keep my thoughts, words and actions as though I was with Baba and He was present with me. Then I would be doing what was His will and not what was my will.

I smiled at Baba. "You never fail to surprise me—You know my thoughts and always try to guide me and put me straight!" Baba's ways are so unfathomable, and I do not know why Baba always answers my doubts, because I am nobody special.

LUCKY DRAW PRIZE:

There was a lucky draw few years back, organised by a Baba lover in the United States, I had made a contribution and was not expecting to win anything. I was going back home from work one day, and once again a strange thought came into my head.

Out of all the people in the world—who are in billions—Baba says that there are only a few hundred who are true lovers of God. So how could Baba know of my existence—that there is a person called Cyrus Bomanji, living in the United Kingdom? I have many weaknesses and flaws and am definitely not a true lover of God, so would Meher Baba even know of my existence?

I was trying to find an answer, so I spoke softly to myself, "Meher Baba, if You know me and recognise me as Cyrus give me a sign." Thinking of a raffle in the United States, I said to Baba, "If I win any raffle item I will take it as a sign that You know me." I was being very foolish, and sometimes I wonder why these ridiculous thoughts come to me.

In the next few days, I got this feeling that I had won something in the raffle even though I did not hear any news from the Baba lover from the United States. However, to my utter surprise and astonishment, I did win a painting of Beloved Baba in the raffle draw!

How fortunate I am! How can I be worthy of His love, even though I keep pestering Him with my childish questions? I thank you my Beloved for having the patience to bear with me and take me through this amazing journey of knowing You.

*****

I was born and raised in Bombay (Mumbai) and now live and work in London for the past several years. I give you my life story, which I have written from the heart: to find, and to spend my entire life under my guiding star—Avatar Meher Baba.

101 Tales of Finding Love

I'M THE ONE, AND I'M BACK

by Kristin Crawford

Meher Baba with Kid, 1938

Kristin Crawford

Kristin Crawford age 13

Krissy and Mom, Meher Center footbridge, January 1974

ay back when I was a small child of about four, I became aware of Jesus. I felt love from Him and for Him and longed to be with Him. I used to sit in my room and make drawings of Jesus. Scribbly though they must have been, my whole heart was in them. In my closet I had a special box where I kept my drawings. I would go outside and pick flowers and grass or leaves to give to Him as offerings in the secret box.

I must have said casually to one of my agnostic parents that I was going to be with Jesus when I grew up, or something to that effect, at which point I was informed that Jesus had lived and died long ago. I was disconsolate with this news. I had a sense that being with Him was the purpose of my life and couldn't believe that I had somehow missed Him. How could things have gone so wrong? I was baffled, and bereft.

In August 1968, when I was twelve, I went with my family to see my cousin, Louise Barrie, who was living in Tennessee. While there, we visited a friend of Louise's, a woman named Francine ("Frankie") Tacker. I have a vague recollection (which only came back to consciousness many years hence) of seeing Baba's name on something lying on a table, perhaps one of the turquoise volumes of the *Discourses*.

Two months went by, and I was now attending an art class that met all day on Saturdays. Sometimes we would go to visit the studios of local artists. On this particular day we went to Woodstock, New York, to the home of an eccentric man named Clarence Schmidt, who had some acres on the mountain overlooking the Ashokan Reservoir. I recall this October 1968 day with an uncanny clarity, including the details of what I was wearing and my mood. I can still see myself getting out of my mother's car that day forty-nine years ago when she dropped me off at the class.

Pieces of sculpture and assorted found objects were hung in the trees or placed along the paths that meandered through the artist's property. I went off by myself to see the art work and explore. Walking on one of the paths, I noticed a photograph of a man's face on a tree perhaps fifteen feet into the woods. The photo seemed to have a magnetic force of its own. As I was taking my first step off the path toward the tree to examine it more closely, I had a marked recognition of Destiny. I felt, "Yes!" I was in the right place at the right time and was taking a step in the direction in which I was meant to go.

As I looked at the image of the man's face ("The Ancient One," it turned out), the photo was no longer a photo. He came alive and was right there before me, not only looking at me, but looking inside me to areas which I did not even know existed. As He gazed at me, and into me, I had a new awareness of my inner being, which extended way beyond my physical body. Suddenly I was huge inside, much bigger than I had ever realized. The inner dimension kept growing as His gaze reached those deep areas inside me, almost as though His gaze itself were expanding that space. He was familiar; I knew Him, and He knew me.

In my mind I heard three things. These exact words came to me unequivocally, as fact:

1) I'm the One, and I'm back;
2) Your life is deeply connected with Me; and
3) When the time is right, you will know more about Me.

I understood. "Oh, it's You!" Nothing could be more natural or simple. There was no need for a debate, no question of accepting or not accepting. I simply knew this was Truth.

Apparently I reported this to my increasingly perplexed parents. My mother tells me that I often mentioned and wondered about this Man, whose name and whereabouts I did not yet know. I wanted to search for Him, but He had kindly reassured me that it would be in His timing.

When I finally did find out more about Baba, He had recently dropped His body. While there was some disappointment at having missed seeing Him with these eyes, how touched I was later to realize that He had reached out to me near the very end of His incarnation, and from Meherazad, the place which became central to my life. But I am getting ahead of myself.

Meanwhile, two years passed. It was 1970, and my cousin, Louise was coming to New York City to see that same friend, Frankie. They were planning to go to a Meher Baba meeting in Greenwich Village. A couple of days before the meeting Louise felt prompted that I was supposed to be there also, and she somehow convinced my parents that I should take the bus to NYC and the subway downtown that Friday afternoon after school, something which my fourteen-year-old self had never done alone (and was thrilled to do). I walked from the subway to Westbeth, where Frankie lived. As soon as I went into Frankie's apartment, I felt elation, which continued as Frankie, Louise and I walked over to Baba House on Barrow Street and took the elevator up to the encounter with the One who had been patiently waiting for us forever.

When we entered the room, a large photo of Baba was straight ahead. Again, this was no ordinary photo! From His enormous eyes, waves of love were radiating out to us. I could not only feel the love but I could see it. It was circulating, surrounding and reaching everyone in the room. Bili Eaton was speaking that night, and I was floating in and on a sea of joy. I was home.

I spent many weekends in the following months in New York, going to Baba House with Frankie. The next big event on my Baba time line was my first trip to the Meher Center, at Easter vacation, 1971. Even though we had an offer of a ride from New York to the Center leaving one day later, that was out of the question—we couldn't possibly wait that long! We instead opted to take the bus from Port Authority.

Arriving at the Myrtle Beach bus station in the evening, we had no idea how to get to the Center. We hopped in a taxi, and the driver drove north through what was then wilderness and eventually, by some miracle, found the entrance. When we passed through the gate, I felt an immediate shift in atmosphere. Fred and Ella Winterfeldt came out of Pine Lodge to hug us, which in itself was worth the eighteen hours on the bus! Fred directed the taxi driver to take us all the way to the cabins, quite an adventure when one does not know the way, in the dark of night. The taxi left us off right by the Lagoon Cabin, and I remember seeing the full moon above and reflected on the lake. I had arrived in Paradise. I believe the date was April 4, 1971, Palm Sunday.

Frankie and I were assigned to the Lantern Cabin, and my cousin Louise joined us there. For all of us, this was the first visit to Beloved Baba's Center, and we spent the week in rapturous states. We met with Elizabeth, who seemed to be attuned to every visitor and every minute detail of the working of the Center. Kitty spent hours with us telling her Baba story and inquiring about ours. Everywhere we met such extraordinary people, radiant with a Joy that now had a name: Meher Baba.

Somehow I continued with my prosaic high school life after this, attending meetings at Baba House when I could, and occasionally at Michael Siegell's place in New Paltz and Tom and Yvonne Riley's in Woodstock. By now the dream on the horizon was to meet the people in India who had lived their lives with Baba. I hatched the idea of doubling up my last two years of high school to make an early escape and have a year off before college. Baba must have arranged everything, because I otherwise cannot imagine how it was possible. Off I went at sixteen, in January 1973, and was welcomed into the sacred garden by His beloved jewels, Mehera, Mani and all the others.

That story goes on and on. What treasure He bestowed through His mandali! Even the ultimate "job," of letting me be near them and help them out (unquestionably it was the other way around) for many years. Now that era is over, and I look back in disbelief at what Baba gave to me, which was beyond my most intrepid wishes. The little four-year-old girl who thought she had missed Jesus-Baba was not disappointed.

*****

I currently live both in New York City and in New Paltz, New York, where I cared for my mother in her home until her death in 2016. By Baba's Grace I continue to spend time every year at Meherazad and am working on various editorial and archival projects.

TRULY HE HAS RETURNED

by Phyllis Craft Crawford

Phyllis Crawford

Sarah, Aloba, Kris, Meherwan, Phyllis, at Meherazad 2002.

Ifirst heard Meher Baba's name in October 1968 when Kris returned from her Saturday art class field trip to Woodstock and excitedly proclaimed that on a tree she had seen the picture of the One she was going to follow all her life. She was then twelve years old, and neither her father nor I considered this announcement as anything but adolescent fantasy. In our agnostic household, religion of any kind was dishonored as superstition. We did not even encourage her to discuss the matter, which we dismissed until sometime later when her cousin, Louise Barrie, had a similar experience. The two girls joined forces, going to meetings in Greenwich Village, one of which we finally consented to attend. To say that no conversion took place is an understatement: we thought it was complete nonsense, from the praising of the strange, silent man's name to the hugging, which we put down as a disguised sexuality. To our credit, however, we did not interfere with Kris' pursuit of Meher Baba, which seemed to be beneficial and to promote associations with good people.

When, at the age of sixteen, and already graduated from high school, Kris made the even more shocking announcement that she was going to Baba's ashram in India, we considered this to be overstepping the bounds of reasonable behavior. She would get no help from us. She didn't expect help. She would earn the money herself, which she did by cleaning houses and making fruit smoothies at a progressive local theater. In January 1973, as I stood crying, she took off on Air India, accompanied by a slightly older Baba lover. During the two months of her absence, my moods alternated between terror that she wouldn't return alive (and the lack of communication in those days wasn't reassuring), and hope that the experience would cure her of this madness. Of course it didn't—and she returned very much alive.

Fast-forward to July 1973, when I had another shock. Kris' father came down to breakfast, said he was leaving to have a "new life" (lower case), and by evening was gone, never to return. All my security—emotional, social, financial—disappeared with him. I was hopeless and helpless, ripe for the entrance of God. As is aptly stated, "There are no atheists in foxholes." And I was really in a foxhole, because that very summer most of the significant people in my life moved away: Kris to college, her sister and family to Sweden, Bob and Sarah Barrie to Virginia, my parents to Florida, and finally, the next year, a man who promised me a new life, to instant death in an auto accident.

Would that I had turned to Baba at that time, or that He had pursued me! But no, I had to take a circuitous route, suffer greatly, and learn many lessons beforehand. I had no dramatic epiphany, just incremental progress. I knew I needed spiritual help but wasn't ready to accept what Baba was offering.

A return to the Episcopal Church in which I was raised and in which I had once been devout was out of the question, as many of the Christian doctrines seemed in error: Virgin Birth, Resurrection, the exclusion of all non-believers from Salvation. Jesus Himself I revered for His teachings, which I still tried to follow. Someone suggested studying the writings of the psychic, Edgar Cayce, which I did enthusiastically for several years. Their chief contribution was a belief in reincarnation as fundamental to the workings of the Universe and as preparation for Baba.

On Krissy's eighteenth birthday, in 1974, I spent a few days with her at the Meher Spiritual Center in Myrtle Beach. I was carried away with the natural beauty of the place, but even more so with the utter devotion to Baba of Elizabeth, Kitty and everyone I met there. Though their stories of how they had come to Him impressed me, I felt no personal call. At home, however, I read the *Discourses* and was intellectually engaged. Difficult as some of them were to understand and to follow, they made sense. For me, this was essential, even though I am inherently a heart- and not mind-based person. I began to attend Baba meetings, but then ten years of caring for my parents took me away from these sources, except for rare occasions with Kris.

The major leap forward occurred in 1990 when Sarah Barrie, my ex-sister-in-law and dearest friend, and I decided that it was past time for us to visit the scene of our daughters' devotion, Meherabad and Meherazad, in India, though the girls were not there at the time. Everyone was very loving and helpful at the Meher Pilgrim Center. With going up the Hill to Baba's Samadhi, spending the days at Meherazad to meet the mandali and basking in the warmth of their love for Baba, listening to Mani and Eruch in Mandali Hall and to Bhau's talks in the Meher Pilgrim Center dining room, we were reeling. In the tranquility of Baba's bedroom, we felt His Presence, and my heart pounded with joy to see there the picture of Jesus, and to realize that He had truly returned as He had promised. This trip was the turning point in both of our spiritual lives. We came, we saw, and Baba conquered.

Sarah and I made three more trips to India, the last one in 2002 with Wendell Brustman, who had become a close friend, and whose epic book, *Live Again for the First Time,* I was helping him to edit. Doing this work under the tutelage of a man whose life was an earnest search for God was a privilege for which I'll always be grateful. Even so, I might not have embarked upon that last trip, at age eighty, but for an extraordinary experience that helped me to make the decision to go. While I lay awake in bed pondering it, Baba Himself came and sat on the bed, beaming at me. He extended His hand to me, and the softness of His skin and the Love coming from Him was like nothing I had ever felt.

Awakening to Baba has caused many changes in my thinking. First of all, it is comforting to know that He is in charge, that the sorrows and losses are given us from His Love, that the events in all of our lives are not random ones but purposeful. As a congenitally anxious person, not to worry is a challenge, but I'm improving! Several other times Baba has come to me, in dreams. Am I too greedy in wishing for this again?

Phyllis Craft Crawford

*****

Phyllis Craft Crawford died peacefully at her home in New Paltz, New York, on April 4, 2016 at age ninety-four and a half. Her daughter Kristin was singing Baba's name to her and daughter Diane was in the next room. Phyllis made one last, lovely trip to the Meher Center in October 2015.

101 Tales of Finding Love

I Am the Lord
of the Universe

by Joe DiSabatino

"Baba at Window," painting by
and © Joe DiSabatino

Joe DiSabatino

I'm nineteen and running down the street full-speed, breaking into the open for a long pass in a game of touch football, my head turned backwards, my eyes fixed on the quarterback, then the ball is arcing high through the air, ready to land in my outstretched hands—and wham! I collide forehead-first into the back of the parked station wagon I had forgotten was there. I'm knocked out for a few seconds and when I come fully around I'm in an ambulance. I still have the scar on my forehead. After that, I become more inward-looking. A few months later I experience divine love for the first time.

It's the summer between my freshman and sophomore years of college, 1966. I'm a night watchman at a small hotel in Ocean City, New Jersey. One evening I'm walking the boardwalk, a few hours to kill before my shift starts. An Afro-American man, obviously drunk, thrusts his hand into my face and asks for some change. My initial instinct is to say no, get away, and keep on walking which I start to do. But something inside makes me stop, turn around and offer to buy him a meal at the diner across the way.

As he gratefully devours the cheeseburger, French fries and hot coffee, a wave of love breaks inside and transforms this stranger, this drunk, into my brother, into myself. Back in my small closet of a room, I stretch out on the bed, still an hour to kill before clocking in. This time wave after wave after wave of oceanic love floods my being for a good twenty minutes. I know the small gift I gave that man was being given back a thousand fold. Who was he? Three years later I am given the same overwhelming experience of divine love, but this time I can name the Source: Meher Baba.

During my last two years of college, I often avoid the student cafeteria lunchtime small talk and head for a botanical garden in a nearby wealthy Main Line Philadelphia neighborhood. I sit on a rock in the middle of a small stream and watch the water course by. Something inside, a still small voice I can't quite identify, is calling me. Not with words but with indecipherable whispers.

When I graduate in June 1969, there is only one thing I want to do: go to California. After sixteen years of Catholic education in New Jersey and Philadelphia, I am ready to cut loose. I have no idea where in California I am going, I'll figure that out when I get there. I drive a destination car to Dallas, then another one to Los Angeles. Once there, I know I should keep going, so I take a bus to San Francisco. When I see the sign at the San Francisco bus terminal that says "Bay Bridge, University of California, Berkeley" I know that's my destination. By the end of the day I am lodged in a student house in Berkeley for the summer.

1969 was the summer after the summer of love. Police on every corner in downtown Berkeley after the People's Park riot, colorful hippies, street music, drugs, head shops, VW van-loads of beaded and bearded people heading cross-country to the Woodstock festival in New York. I feel totally at home there in a way I never had on the East coast.

One day during my first week in Berkeley I stroll past a cheese shop. A "Don't Worry, Be Happy" poster in the window with a photo of a smiling man named Meher Baba catches my attention. That is the first time I see him and read his name. There is something *alive* and warmly engaging about the photo. I make a point of walking past the cheese shop whenever I can, smiling back or winking at this happy man. Is he a baker, a Greek cheese-maker? Whatever—his smile makes me smile inside.

Someone moves out, so we need a new housemate. We pin a card on the community board and somebody named Ray D'Argenio from the Bronx shows up and takes the room. Ray and I hit it off like brothers, two East coast Italians in search of the Truth and adventure. He has Meher Baba's *Discourses* and strongly encourages me to read them. I soon discover that this man Meher Baba has a lot more to say about life and the spiritual path than "Don't Worry, Be Happy."

94

I devour the *Discourses*. I remember thinking, "This man knows from direct experience what He is talking about. He is not just philosophizing." The vibrating truth of Baba's words plumbs deep down inside me and resonates all day and all night like a cathedral bell. I went to a Jesuit college, and so read the major Catholic theologians, the history of Western philosophy, and a Zen book or two by Alan Watts. That was it—I'm not seeking a guru, not into yoga or anything Eastern. That summer I do three LSD trips, each different and seemingly enlightening. I'm starting to enjoy the drug.

In the first week of August, 1969, I attend a Meher Baba meeting on campus. I enter the auditorium and everyone seems familiar to me. Still shy and in awe of the Berkeley culture, I sit in the back and don't say a word to anyone. The person leading the meeting introduces Meher Baba, says a few words about His life and Avataric claim. What he is saying makes perfect sense to me. Then he shows a film of Baba.

I don't recall which film it was. When I see Baba come to life on the screen, I instantly fall head-over-heels in love with Him. I know Him, I know He is who and what I had been unconsciously seeking for the past three years. Quietly, in the back row of the auditorium, I experience an overpowering joyful reunion with my true Beloved as wave after wave after wave of divine love, as it had at the New Jersey beach three years prior, sweep through me. For the next three months or so I walk or rather float two feet off the ground on a sustained Baba honeymoon.

People on the street in Berkeley stop me and comment on the "beautiful vibe" I am emanating. No one has ever said that to me. I want to say, "It's not me, it's Him." One sunny day I walk past a restaurant window on Telegraph Avenue and the waitress inside, who has her back to me while wiping a table, turns and beams a loving smile like we are old friends. The sidewalk, the trees, the clouds, in fact all objects in the external world glow with His radiant divine presence. Inside, I can feel and even taste and see, when I close my eyes, Baba's same loving presence lighting up the cells of my body, head to foot.

Some days I sit for hours on a bench or at the fountain at Sproul Plaza on campus, content to simply be with Him inside and outside. Other days I hang out at a bookstore on Telegraph Avenue, eagerly reading *The God Man* by Charles Purdom and *Avatar* by Jean Adriel. I come across the pamphlet "God in a Pill," Baba's warning about the dangers of LSD and other drug use. I make up my mind to stop all drug use, including marijuana. Baba saves me from going off the deep end with LSD since, after three enjoyable acid trips in June and July, I was planning to keep using it.

One day in late August I sense that He wants me to go off where I can be alone. So I walk up into the Berkeley hills and find a small but elegant botanical garden with a blue bench and a view of the bay in the distance. I sit down and enjoy the bird song, the smells of flowers on the breeze. Then I hear a voice inside, clear as the summer sky, speak these words to me: *"Do not think of yourself in any way. Do for others and you do for Me. Love Me more and more."*

On that day and ever since I'm puzzled as to why Baba bothered giving me the first directive. Surely, He knows that one is impossible. At least directives two and three are doable. But perhaps assigning an impossible task makes the first directive closest to His way. After all, no one except Mehera loved Him as He ought to be loved, but He still encourages us to keep trying.

I look for a job in Berkeley and fail. The job counselor says, "You and fifty thousand other people your age want to find work here. What marketable skills do you have?"

I graduated with a degree in English literature, so I smiled and said, "Thanks, anyway."

In October, running out of money, Ray and I drive back East in his 1960 Studebaker station wagon. Ray drops me off at my house in South Jersey, meets my parents who are grateful to have me back in one piece, then he heads home to New York City. Meher Baba and the "Don't Worry, Be Happy" poster on my bedroom wall were not well-received at home. I immediately find a job as a welfare caseworker in Camden, New Jersey. By this time, three or four months after my August reunion with Him, the Baba honeymoon high is starting to wear off, being back in New Jersey accelerating the return to earth, I'm sure. But my bonding with Baba slowly deepens and solidifies as I connect with Baba lovers in the Philadelphia area—the inimitable Bob Brown is the first person I meet. He works as a zookeeper in Hersey, Pennsylvania, singing Baba's praises to the monkeys and llamas and any other animal or human who would listen.

I have been saying His Name internally since early August, before I read that He wants His lovers to do that. It just happens spontaneously, as if He is repeating His own Name through me. I go the Meher Center in Myrtle Beach, South Carolina for the first time at Easter, 1970. I meet Kitty, Elizabeth and Jane and fall in love and awe with the Center and the three of them. Back in November of '69, one unforgettable night I have my one and only Baba dream.

In November, I had not been to the Meher Center yet, nor had I seen photos of the place. In my dream, I am wandering along a dusty path for lifetimes. I come to the top of a low hill and spy a brick house surrounded by a tall wooden fence in the vale below. I immediately know that is my long-sought destination. Excited, I rush down the hill, and enter the open gate with the name "Meher Abode" carved on a small wooden plaque on the fence next to the gate. (In the dream, it's Baba's house exactly as it really is, down to the smallest details).

I feel so happy to be here! I enter the compound and admire the garden. I keep walking straight to the porch where I remove my shoes. I step into the living room and am surprised to find a group of Westerners and Easterners inside. They are all waiting for Baba to arrive. Every detail in the living room is the way it is in real life except for one thing: there's a TV and the Westerners are watching it. I think, "How in the world can they watch TV when Baba is about to arrive?" Meanwhile the Eastern lovers in the room are arranged in two parallel lines. They are poor villagers and are singing a song of praise to Baba while bobbing up and down, some beating drums as they do so.

Much later, I see the Arangaon villagers next to Meherabad doing the exact same dance in a Baba film, but at that point in my life I had never seen it. I join them, chanting Baba's Name, while beating a drum and happily bobbing up and down with them. Finally He arrives. Baba is wearing a beautiful pink coat, just as He did at the Meher Center in 1952. I see glowing lines of love energy radiating out from His heart to every heart in the room. I can see and feel His love-line piercing my heart. It's as if He's the hub and the love-lines spokes of a wheel. I experience myself as a small chunk of iron and He a powerful, irresistible magnet.

Internally, I 'hear' Him say He wants someone to tell Him a joke. Someone obliges with a really corny one, Baba laughs silently and heartily, with open hand gestures and sparkling eyes. Then I suddenly hear Him say, "Follow Me." He walks through the living room doorway and into the hall leading to His bedroom. I follow and, soon as I cross the threshold, I'm instantly in a whole new place.

I'm now in outer space, seated next to Baba. He's sitting in a chair similar to the one in Mandali Hall at Meherazad. There is no floor per se but somehow the black, empty space is supporting His chair and my body. I gaze out and see the entire physical universe spread out at His feet. The scene resembles a deep space photo from the Hubble telescope.

I then realize the thinking part of my mind has stopped. No more thoughts, the monkey mind gone, obliterated. Just feeling—indescribable love for and from Baba, deep imperturbable peace, and unshakeable contentment prevail. I know I can sit there next to Him in that state for all eternity and never desire anything more.

Then Baba makes a sweeping gesture with His right arm and hand, indicating the countless galaxies and nebulae at His feet. I hear Him say, *"See, I am the Lord of the universe."*

I wake up. It's four a.m. Tears stream down my face from having just met and spent time with Baba—both in this world and somewhere in His. I want to run outside and yell, "Wake up, world! Meher Baba is the Lord of the universe!"

*****

Joe DiSabatino lives in Myrtle Beach, South Carolina. A retired psychotherapist, Joe spends his time painting, writing and directing Baba plays, teaching Art Appreciation courses, and leading Mindfulness meditation classes and workshops.

101 Tales of Finding Love

MY BABA GROOMING

by Jill English

Meher Baba, the Ancient One 1925

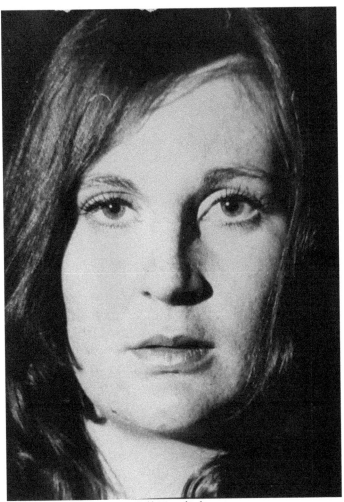

Jill English

The phone was ringing off the hook as I dumped my armload of textbooks onto the kitchen table to free a hand to answer. "Hey, you've got to come over and meet this guy. We're making fresh strawberry daiquiris—and bring one of your joints."

"I can't, I've got too much homework and finals are coming up."

"I'm telling you, you'll be happy you did, so just do it."

"Okaaay Carol," I replied with a long sigh of resignation. I knew why she really called. I could tell it in the tone and inflection of her voice. She wanted to throw me some business. She had a significant stash of pot already so I knew she didn't need it. However, dealing weed was how I was providing for my two young children while also putting myself through university.

I had just divorced my psychopath husband, who was dangerous, violent, and proudly psychologically abusive. It was the early seventies, so police were light on domestic violence. Ultimately, the court issued a permanent restraining order against my ex with the stipulation that he never come within three hundred feet of me or my kids again. But that's another story within the story, yet still must be considered as part of the grooming Baba was orchestrating to bring me to Him.

Carol was my neighbor from the apartment building across the alley. I used to babysit her kid on the nights she worked as a stripper and hooker. I knew this must be one of her good customers, and she wanted to share. I had trouble focusing anyway, so Carol provided an attractive distraction. Off I went with a big joint knowing that I was about to expand my customer base. I always needed money, but I was very selective to whom I sold. Being a woman weed dealer was not all that common back then, but I had good connections that would 'front' me product.

Carol's client, whose name you don't need to know—unless you already do—who is also long dead, shall not be mentioned. But he became one of my best customers of all time, and the one who first spoke Meher Baba's name to me, a lot, ad nauseam, bringing books, pictures and stories of his times in San Francisco with Sufism Reoriented and Ivy O. Duce, that would promptly get put in a corner somewhere in my house or mind. To me, the way he treated his family, justified his disgusting behavior with his very sharp intelligence, education, and wit, as well as how bought his many girlfriends, did not make the Meher Baba he was selling very appealing to me at all. But he wasn't the one who closed that deal. No. It was impossible for me to take him seriously under such blaring hypocrisies.

It was his ongoing relationship with Don Stevens, a very formidable person of stature (in many ways) that became intriguing to me. He told so many stories of Don Stevens, that when Don came to Denver I was already dying to meet him. And so I did, in an open Baba meeting that was manipulated by my customer to happen at MY house one evening, followed by a private dinner on another in 1976, and where after making a snide remark about talking straight to God without going through some guru at the open Baba meeting, I became thoroughly smitten with Don Stevens—the quintessentially kind, loving ambassador of Baba, with his keen insights, and gentle, relentless honesty.

Don Stevens actually made me feel genuinely accepted right away, like he was truly interested in me as a person, with all the fear and painful drama that I was towing with every footstep, despite my rude remark. Well, after THAT kind of encounter, and almost immediately, I wanted to be the person that Don reflected back to me from his eyes. I wanted to recognize that person as me, and put my best foot forward for Don. I wanted to change for Don because I wanted to continue to feel his love. It most certainly didn't happen overnight, and is still unfolding—probably forever.

For decades I always thought that the reason Don was so loving and accepting, although very stern at times, with my customer, was because Mr. Customer was so adept at hiding his stinky traits. But that wasn't it at all. Even Don had become victim to some of the customer's deranged thinking. It was because Don so loved his master, Meher Baba, that he sought to love that one-ness, that Baba, that lies within us all. He was wanting to be the person that Baba's eyes loved, just like I wanted to be the person that Don saw in me. How could I resist that? How could I ignore that warmth and acceptance? I had to seek the source of it. Don Stevens gave me no choice but to plunge into a face-to-face, albeit tumultuous, yet infinite relationship with our divine master, Me-her Baba.

Ah, but there's more! Really, because of Don Stevens I have been invited to submit this story. In the thinking about it, remember-ing a lot of heavy past, I see a little better how Baba is only love, and how He loves us all no matter what our shortcomings, stinky characteristics, eccentricities, and our almost continual judgment of ourselves and judgment of others. In a thought to myself I ask, "Why do we always have to become 'better than,' make someone else 'less than' just because they don't agree or do things the way we think?" Baba LOVES Mr. Customer. He LOVES my psycho-pathic ex. He even LOVES all the Baba lovers who I might think are stupid, or imperious, or hypocrites, or boring or lame. Baba loves us ALL, so He never stops giving us opportunities to for-give. He already has forgiven anyone who has ever done anything 'wrong' anywhere, because He is only Love. He loves us so much that He gives us the freedom to continually repeat our stinky pat-terns, eternally if we so desire, until we forgive (and act on it, ac-cording to Don). Forgiveness is love, love is forgiveness—simple, but very hard.

So Baba has been grooming me to become a forgiver. Mr. Cus-tomer and I have possibly also been His instrument, in my opin-ion, in the grooming of Carol (who, by the way, served time in prison for shooting her boyfriend, Duck, five times the day after he had slapped her so hard it knocked her wig across the room during a party at my house the night before. Duck did not die). Maybe I was also His instrument in the beginning stages of His grooming of my ex. After all, I have two children by him. Carol wanted, thoughtfully, to help enhance my life. Is all this because of that? Is this the butterfly effect of forgiveness? In fact, I feel the telling of this story is another opportunity to refine my grooming experience.

Jai Baba!

*****

I live in Westminster, Colorado.

Because I'm still being groomed by Baba and the memory of Don Stevens, who wanted to have pilgrimage ongoing throughout the United States, I am part of an amazing team of six who have established a non-profit: The Heartland Project—reconnecting humanity like beads on one string. Baba seems to be continuing to use me as His tool, or spiritual worker if you will, because there is only one other Baba lover on this team. The other four, two of which are icon Freedom Riders from the Civil Rights Movement of the sixties, and two of which are Cherokee women from the Cherokee Coalition of Healing and Wellness, fell in love with Baba's message of beads on one string. Our mission is all about forgiveness and reconciliation, through pilgrimage and other means. Baba's name is being spoken to many other people now, people who likely would never have heard it in this life. Please see us on Facebook.

101 Tales of Finding Love

Now You Have To Help Me

by Tim Garvin

Tim Garvin at Sarosh Canteen, Ahmednagar 1980

Tim Garvin

Tim and Eruch, Meherazad, early 1990s

I first heard Meher Baba's name in 1967 on "The Joe Pyne Show." Joe Pyne was a television personality, and he was the insult host of the day. His guests were Rick Chapman and Allan Cohen, two young Americans who had been in communication with Baba (Rick had been in India with Baba, and Baba and Allan had been corresponding). Their message to the world from Baba was "Don't take drugs," and Joe was interviewing them.

Every time "The Joe Pyne Show" came on, you'd stop to see if he was going to say something obnoxious. At the time—I was nineteen—I was not searching for God. I wasn't sure there was a God. I was reading philosophy, but I wasn't sure about God. But I was definitely interested in the inner being and what the truth of life was, so when I heard these guys had just come from a guy who may know what the truth is, I stopped and listened. They showed a picture of Meher Baba and gave his message about the harm that drugs can do. What was so interesting about that show was that it was the only Joe Pyne show I ever saw that Joe didn't insult the guests. He was very respectful, and here you'd think that these guys from India with a guru, someone other than Jesus, he's really going to hammer them. But he was very respectful. (Not long after, Joe Pyne had a heart attack and died.)

That was the single biggest impression I took away from that show—he did not insult them. I met Rick Chapman later in India, and he said, "Yes, that was extraordinary." Anyway, I heard Baba's name before he dropped the body, and I have always been grateful for that.

Three years later, in 1969, I was in college at Louisiana State University, restless, taking philosophy classes. I was trying to understand my own life, grappling with philosophy to increase my understanding of myself and what it was to be in the moment and be a human being. It was difficult because philosophy is a historical conversation written by people who view life through a highly intellectual lens, and you have to be a real scholar to get anywhere, and even then, where are you? Lost in a forest of thought. And it was so tedious, since all I really wanted was to understand myself and life and know the truth, to get to the bottom of what life is, to know why are we here.

I had the experience many times of being involved in some philosophical tussle like, for instance, the dilemma of determinism and free will, and I would browse bookstores, looking at titles, and reading at random almost. Then somehow I'd pick up a book and land exactly on somebody's explication of just the problem I had been deliberating. And I'd say, wow, this guy's saying just what I concluded myself, or near enough, and then suddenly I would experience an overwhelming ennui, almost despair. So that problem is solved and neatly dispatched, and still my heart aches, and the loneliness doesn't go away. I have to say, that was grippingly poignant for me as a young man without any guidance, without any mentor. None of us get that, really, when we're young unless you accept some religion. You just have to hack something out of the chaos. There's no teepee down by the river where you can go talk to the chief. Because nobody really knows anything.

But those days, the days of my youth, were full of egotism and girls and also some dabbling in drugs. Of course this was in the sixties, a wild time. I was not taking hard drugs, but I was taking grass and LSD occasionally. But then through LSD I became aware that there was a reality far beyond the reality of my surface world. So I really became interested in God and spirituality, and I began to read the testimonies of saints.

And I stumbled onto the work of Aurobindo Ghose. In fact, Aurobindo Ghose is still a great part of my thinking. Though he is still mostly ignored, I think he was the preeminent spiritual scholar-poet-critic of the twentieth century. I don't know of anyone in the world of letters whom I have a higher regard for than Aurobindo Ghose. I have his complete works. He's mentally brilliant and well-educated, but also a sixth plane saint, according to Baba, and his writing gives a structure to the world much the same as Baba's but with more analytic detail and excursions into politics, sociology, philosophy, literary criticism. It is said that Baba gave him realization after Aurobindo dropped the body. In any case, he helped purify my intellect and gave me a better ability to think about the human psyche. Also during that time, I read the *Gita,* Mahendranath Gupta's biography of Ramakrishna, *The Gospel of Sri Ramakrishna*—I just pored through that section of the LSU library.

At this point I had dropped out of college for a bit and was living on a farm in Gross Tête, Louisiana near Baton Rouge with a friend of mine, who later died of AIDS from shooting drugs. His wife died too. I was completely frustrated with my search for God. I was looking for a guru, dedicated to finding a guru. This relates to my disgust with philosophy, and to a lot of what follows—because I thought I needed a personal master nearby who could say, "Here's how you dress and behave, and here's the chant. And here's how to meditate." Whatever masters did. I didn't know what they did, but I knew they did something because all the books talked about masters. So I thought, "Well, that's what I need." I went down to New Orleans once to look for this supposed master who was actually a complete fraud. It was funny really—I went to see her, and she was gone, but her chief disciple allowed me to come into the French Quarter ashram they had there. We were sitting at a table, and I think he was nervous and didn't have a lot to say, and suddenly he burst out with a long, extremely loud "Om." Right in my face. Funny now, but unnerving then.

Anyway, I was frustrated and full of restlessness that I couldn't find a master. It was like there was this big knot in my mind, and I couldn't find the end of the rope. That's all we need, the end of the rope, and that's what Baba gives us. But I couldn't find the end of that rope. I was maddened by this inability to do anything. I meditated and had various experiences of a psychic nature, but in the end they were outside the knot and not useful, just as Baba tells us. So one morning I had an inspiration—and I went outside and picked up a log and carried it through the woods. An aspiration had welled up within me and was directed toward the Almighty whom I didn't know anything about, and whom I couldn't reach and get a grip on. So I carried the log and said, "This is all I can give you. I can't the find the end to unravel this knot. Now you have to help me. I'm like an ox. I'm a beast of burden. I have nothing else. I'm out of ideas." The next day I'd get up and go get the log and carry it back.

Then a friend of mine got a job as a camp counselor in Massachusetts, so I called the camp and also got a job there. On my way north, I stopped in Pittsburgh to visit my old friend, Carl Berreckman, my philosophy professor at LSU, who was now teaching at Duquesne. Carl had a buddy who was a psychology professor named Rolf, and we went over to Rolf's house to visit. And Rolf had a friend and protégé named Lawrence Reiter. He was living with Rolf. Lawrence and I talked, and he told me he was devoted to Meher Baba, a master who had just dropped his body in India.

So we talked and talked, and he gave me a book called *The Everything and the Nothing*. But at the time it was just one of the many books I had. I had *The Tibetan Book of the Dead*, the *Gita*, *Krishnamurti*, *The Autobiography of a Yogi*— all those books that come your way. Besides, Meher Baba was dead, or so I thought. I didn't know it then, but the cry my heart had uttered when I was carrying the log had been answered.

So I left Pittsburgh and went to be a camp counselor for the summer—the summer of the moon landing [1969]. I read the book, and in my ignorance wondered what spiritual plane I was on. Maybe the third, maybe the second, except I couldn't do miracles. In any case, it was all in my head and not useful. And Baba was dead.

Skip ahead to the next winter, in December of 1970. I went back to Pittsburgh to visit, and again we went over to Rolf's house. And there was Lawrence again. Again we talked and talked, and Lawrence, who was a great fan of Poe's, read some poems. As I recall it, there was some ego involved on both sides, he and I, young men competing in ideas and attitudes. But he had just come from the Meher Center, and I think he was feeling rapturous, and at the end of that evening, something amazing happened, and this is on the dot the moment I became a Baba lover. We were standing in the hallway saying goodbye. Lawrence, with whom I had been intellectually arm-wrestling a moment before, embraced me and said very feelingly, "You should think about Meher Baba." And somehow the barriers were gone, and a pulse of love passed between us. Actually, it awakened me. It was a spiritual-psychic thing. I felt, "Oh! That's right!" I felt love enter my heart center. That's what I had been wanting all my life. Baba says about love that those who don't have it catch it from those who do, and in my case that's how it happened.

The next day I got on a bus to the Meher Center. Then I was on my honeymoon. I read the books, the *Discourses*, and everything you do when you first come. Bob Brown was there, and we became friends. He told me what *sanskaras* were.

I was broke, so I'd make a big pot of lentil stew, and leave it in the refrigerator for days and eat on it. Of course, I wasn't the only one who ate it. Lots of kitchen scavengers in those days! I stayed there for a couple of weeks, and then I was thrown off because I had drugs with me. I had told someone, and he told Jane Haynes, who was in charge of the Center while Kitty and Elizabeth were in India. Jane called me and said, "Do you have drugs?"

I said "Yes." I had hidden them in the woods. I had this tiny stash of drugs, either LSD or STP, which I had gotten in San Francisco months earlier. I was not taking drugs then, but I still had this little stash and had taken them to Pittsburgh in hopes of finding someone to sell them to. So Jane said I had to leave. And I'm in love with Meher Baba! It was as if life had opened my throat and was just pouring this information, this nectar of Divinity into me and slam, throat closed! I was actually hugging trees. I would experience a tree. I'd go off into the woods, and I would just feel.

So I left the Center, went back to Baton Rouge, and sold those drugs to somebody. I took the money I got, not much, but enough for a bus ticket, and a week later I was on a bus going back to the Center. I got to Atlanta and called Jane from a phone booth. I said, "This is Tim Garvin. Remember me? I'm the guy who had the drugs."

"Yes, yes," she said.

"Well, I'm on my way back."

She said, "Elizabeth and Kitty are not here yet, and I have to consult them before I can permit you to return."

"Jane, I'm begging you. Meher Baba is everything to me now." And so she consented. I have always been grateful to her for the faith and courage she showed in permitting this unknown drug addict to return.

I went back to the Center, and I stayed a long time, a month or two. Various other people were there, but it was early days, and the Center was mostly empty. I had some interesting experiences, and as Baba says, these experiences served to confirm my faith and understanding, but are not something important in themselves. I was out in the Boathouse one night, and I saw this little image of Baba's face out in the distance, maybe one hundred yards away. Everywhere I'd look, that picture would be there. Later on, I read *Listen, Humanity,* and found that during the East-West Sahavas Baba told a gathering of men, "Some of you will see Me tonight. You will see a small image of me in the distance." That's what I had seen.

This was in 1971, and Kitty and Elizabeth returned from India where they had been visiting. We were introduced by Jane, and of course they inquired about the drugs and were satisfied that I was free of them. Shortly afterwards, Adi K. Irani came to the States and stayed at the Center. I had long discussions with him.

I was still a student of Aurobindo, and I asked Adi, "Why do I need Meher Baba? Why not just God? How can Meher Baba help me?"

And Adi said, "Oh brother, you don't need Baba. Don't believe in Baba if you don't want to."

I said "No! no! I love Baba! I want to know how he can help."

I remember John Bass, one of the old New York Baba lovers, finally said impatiently, "Tell him to read *God Speaks*. Has he read *God Speaks*?"

But Adi defended me. It so happened that Adi too was interested in Aurobindo's writings. In fact he told me he once had a book of Aurobindo's and was carrying it around Meherazad one day, and Baba called him and took the book and said, "You don't need Aurobindo. You have Me." But the next day he gave it back to him. I had lots of questions for Adi, and he patiently tried to answer them.

But the interesting part of my story at that time is that though I loved Baba and everything he said, he had dropped his body. He was gone. So how can he be my master? But Adi said, "Baba is the eternal master and available everywhere for all time."

I said, "Baba said that? Where does He say that? Show me where it is in the books." He couldn't.

Kitty couldn't either. She said, "I read it,"

I said, "But where?" Somehow she couldn't say.

Adi said, "He's always awake to the world. He drops the physical body, but His universal body never drops."

I said, "Where does it say that?" I drove him crazy. I would say, "What's the use of Baba? What leverage can He provide to pry this ego away?"

Finally, he said, "He can provide this. He comes and becomes the focal point of the universe. His name, His photograph. It all condenses into a focal point, and is a source of divine yoga sanskaras which you can then imbibe. That's the use of Meher Baba in the world." I liked that explanation, and it has become a commanding concept for me in explaining to myself and others why Baba is useful, why he's not just a body of thought or a religious figurehead. He's a living force of divine sanskaras within each of us. But still, in my restless youth, I was not completely at ease. After all, where in the writing did it say precisely that? Adi did his best, but there was still something in me which longed for more clarification.

So then I heard about Murshida Ivy Duce out in San Francisco. She had a group out there—Sufism Reoriented. And she was a living master! So I thought I would go out there and talk to her. Shortly after I got married in '71, my wife and I drove a Vespa motor scooter, packed with a tent, two sleeping bags, a duffle, and a guitar, two thousand miles to San Francisco.

At first I spoke to the preceptors, Aneece Hasseen and Lud Dimpfl, and then finally got to see the Murshida. She invited me up to her apartment one evening. She opened the door, and since I didn't know what she looked like, I walked right past her, thinking she was the maid answering the door. Then I looked around and realized, "That's her!" So we sat down and talked. Among other things, she told me to get my astrology chart done by Sylvia DeLong. Murshida had written a book called *What Am I Doing Here?* and in it she had written a sentence, "Those who so blithely think they can follow the inner guide are deluding themselves."

So I said, "What's this about a personal master? Is it really necessary?"

And she said, "Yes, you have to have a personal master."

I said, "But I spoke to Adi about that, and he said you didn't. He said that Baba was the eternal master for all."

She said, "You must have misunderstood him." Crash! Here I am, with Baba for only about a year, and now I find the experts disagree. It was maddening. It was heartbreaking.

I went back to the Center and talked to Kitty. I asked her again, "Do you have to have a personal master?"

She said, "No. Baba is the Avatar, and the Avatar is the Eternal Master."

Again I asked, "Where does it say that, Kitty? Can you find it in the writing?"

Again she said, "I don't know," but she thought she had definitely read it.

I said, "I went to see Murshida Duce, and she said a personal master in the flesh was definitely needed." Kitty was a bit dismayed by this announcement but continued to assert that a personal master was unnecessary once a soul had come into contact with the Avatar.

Jump forward to 1980 and my first trip to India. It was the year of the upheaval between Eruch and the Sufis. I was in Mandali Hall when Eruch first read out his general letter to the Baba community in which he deplored the current focus on spiritualism and occultism, particularly in Sufism Reoriented and the Vedanta movement.

He emphasized that we should remember Baba as the sole focus of our devotion and not get lost in or attracted to occultism. It created a lot of havoc and hurt feelings, and the Sufis came in a delegation to defend themselves. But Eruch was firm and clear.

And Eruch is our Peter, the rock on which our "church" will be founded. Those who knew him and those who have seen him in video will remember his loving but manly selflessness. He was like the touchstone of all that it is to be a true man, a human being. He was a saint no doubt. The scent of his body was saintly.

And of course, now that I had Baba's great spokesman before me, I asked about the need for a personal master. And that, in essence, was what the whole blowup with the Sufis was about. If Baba is dead and out of touch, then we need these secondary people to advise and guide us, and they, being finite, naturally tend to get involved in inner details, and so arises spiritualism. So Eruch had someone go to get a certain article, and Eruch asked me and another man next to me read it out loud in the hall.

> It was written by a Baba lover whose aunt had gone to Bombay to see the chargeman of Bombay, a high saint. When she walked up to him, he said, "Get out of here, you whore!"
>
> So she rushed away, and when she saw Baba, she said, "The chargeman of Bombay harangued me and called me a whore."
>
> Baba said, "Go back to him. He's a great soul." So she went back, and as she drew near, she was of course full of fear.
>
> But the saint said, "Mother, come sit here." And he stroked her hair and was kind to her. He said, "Now you have permission."
>
> She went back to Baba, and Baba said, "You see?"
>
> And the young man writing the article went on to say, "When you come to Baba He is your master. We only need Baba."

And Eruch had me read that out in Mandali Hall to solidify my belief, to give me one more dose of the truth. But I still had doubt, because the article didn't say what to do after Baba dies.

But that was golden time with Eruch. We used to go on little walks with him. Beautiful. I am so grateful for that.

The next time I came to India was in '83. On my first day in Mandali Hall, after the greetings, Eruch began the session with us by remarking to Davana, "Did you find that article?"

She said, "Yes, I found it," and handed him some papers.

Eruch handed them to me and said, "Tim, you have a big strong voice. You read it." I began to read it, and after a few sentences found it was the same article I had heard read out some years earlier. The discussion in the hall the previous day had led Eruch to think of the article for the first time in years. After finishing the article, I told Eruch the whole story of my search, my doubt, and the first reading of the article.

He said, "Brother, we have no idea how He works." The last vestige of doubt about whether I needed a personal master, about Baba's use to us after he drops his physical body, was gone. Baba has dropped His physical body but the body that counts He never drops. Looking back, I can see that this concept was in the writings and in Baba's many messages all along: "I never come, I never go." "I am not this body you see." And most fully in *Avatar of the Age Meher Baba Manifesting*, written by Bhau from notes Baba gave him. But to get it into my hard head, it seems, he had to trouble Eruch.

*****

Now my wife, Cynthia Drake, and I live in the countryside near Durham, NC, where we tend a garden, chickens, and our dog, Blue. I write novels, and Cynthia is working on a grandparent's manual, entitled "*A Trip to Grandmother's.*" Also, in ceramics, using the millefiori technique, I'm currently constructing the seven symbols of the world's religions to be installed in the Memorial Tower in Meherabad, India later in 2017.

101 Tales of Finding Love

A Journey from Seeking Truth to Finding Love

or

The Man with the
Big Moustache Who Said
He Was God

by Aude Gotto

This painting was commissioned as the hanging sign for a Centre for the Arts named The King of Hearts, which I opened in Norwich, England, in 1990. As Meher Baba was the "incognito" inspiration for the name and ethos of the place, the brief given to the artist, with many photographs of Baba, was that the face should not be a straight portrait, but recognisable by anyone who knew Baba; to other people, it should be just a welcoming face, full of affectionate fun. The style, of an old tapestry, was dictated by the fact that the building was a 16th century merchant house.

The famous card.

Baba arrived in my life in a most unexpected way, like a thunderclap in a blue sky, and went straight to the main point: He was God, he said, and I believed him without question, which was completely out of character.

I was then in my early thirties, and for much of my childhood and adolescence, I had made great efforts to feel a personal relationship with Jesus, without any success. I had finally given up trying to find a 'personal' God, and decided that the way for me was to experience God in the starry sky and in the trees, with which I felt a strong emotive connection, and I was quite satisfied with this.

So I was happily settled with my vision of God in stars and trees, I wasn't searching for anything else, when suddenly Baba arrived in my life, saying that he was God in human form. What a statement!

This took the shape of a small picture, which fell out of a letter explaining that Meher Baba said he was God, and containing various quotes and anecdotes. With his big nose, big moustache, big grin, he did not at all look like what I thought a godly person would be, let alone God Himself. Nevertheless, to my surprise and amazement, I believed him. Something in me said, "This is a man who speaks the Truth."

What had prepared me for this astonishing encounter?

That summer I had been to a workshop centering around the work of psychotherapist Carl Rogers. Among the participants were Michael Da Costa, a counsellor at the University of East Anglia in Norwich, and his colleague Brian Thorne. One afternoon, Michael read aloud his recently written piece, "Frail Love Tokens," which was dedicated to Meher Baba. I was very struck by it, and one line particularly held me through its affirmation of

Oneness: "Is there anything that God isn't?" I thought, "Yes, *this* is what I am looking for."

I wanted to know more about this Meher Baba but I hesitated to ask Michael   directly as I had not met him before and felt this was deeply important to him. I didn't want to get too intense, probably fearing indoctrination. So later on, having tea with Brian, whom I knew well, I asked him, "Who is this Meher Baba that Michael is so keen on?"

The reply startled me, "Well, it is someone who said he was God." The next sentence startled me even more, "This sounds rather like somebody else I know." Brian was a devoted Christian so I knew he meant Jesus. And then even more startling, "Therefore it strikes me as quite plausible." Such a statement from the mouth of a dedicated Christian was so implausible that it really got me hooked. I still believe that Brian never said this sentence—Baba put it in his mouth.

Since childhood I had struggled with the idea that God had only come once, had only one Son, and that all other religions were inferior to Christianity. It seemed somehow unworthy of God to be so limited and to leave so many people out in the cold.

After I got home I decided to write to Michael and ask, "Who is Meher Baba?"

The reply came as a long letter containing the small picture that turned out to be such dynamite!

So, on a summer's day in 1977, I was sitting in my kitchen on my own, holding this little picture and the letter containing many striking quotes and funny anecdotes about Meher Baba; I was weeping and laughing all at the same time, and I just knew that he was who he said he was. I really had no idea what it could mean for a human being to be God, I had always had difficulty with the concept of the Incarnation. My mind said I should feel this was completely ridiculous, but what I actually experienced was that it was totally obvious. There was no space for doubt—I found myself believing totally that Baba was God. It was like recognising an old friend.

Other things contributed to this conviction. On the other side of the grinning picture, there was a smaller photograph next to the quote, "To penetrate into the essence of all being and significance," and I was trying to read this quote, but the eyes of that small photo would not let go of mine. And I heard in my head, "These are the eyes of a man who is alive." I had just read in the letter that Meher Baba had died in 1969, eight years earlier.

Then my rational self had to argue, "Maybe he is indeed a very holy person, and he has just overstepped the mark a bit thinking he is God." The answer came immediately: looking at the grin, the nose, the moustache, the words in my head were, "This man is quite incapable of taking himself seriously; so if he says he is God, then that is what he is."

Other thoughts started flooding in. "So this is what Jesus was talking about, this is the meaning of the 'Incarnation': a man who is God." All of a sudden the concept I had struggled with for years became quite clear and obvious.

The last obstacle was that I was did not see myself as someone who ran after Eastern gurus, I disapproved of that modern trend; was I going to get stuck into some sort of sect? Again Baba provided the answer, through his statement that hypocrisy was the worst sin, "So if you don't believe what I say, then for God's sake don't pretend to." This reassured me that with such a guide I was totally safe: I wasn't going to have to let go of my judgment, to believe what I didn't believe, and it was wonderful that this man who said He was God was not at all concerned whether one believed him or not. It sounded so different from the cross and petty Christian God who got very upset and angry if you didn't go along with all the tenets of the Creed. There was a spaciousness, a freedom here, and on top of it there was FUN: this God-man was not pompous, he liked a laugh, and he even cheated at cards! I was won over: I could follow him, and if I didn't believe some of what he said, I could put it aside until I did.

If I look back on my life to see what led to this moment, I feel that Baba's hand was on me all the way, all through my childhood and growing up, until he finally revealed himself at that crucial moment in my early thirties.

I was born in a Christian family and the existence of God was never in question. My parents both had a genuine faith that informed their behaviour and way of life, but they were never boasting in their beliefs. Total honesty and caring for others was what God was about, and that is how one lived.

My grandmother was a different proposition altogether; she had had a conversion 'experience' and was a staunch, 'born again' evangelist, who believed in the Last Judgement, when some would be saved (she was of course one of those), and others would be thrown out into the darkness where there was "weeping and gnashing of teeth." It was made fairly clear to me that as I was a rather naughty little girl I would not be on the side of the saved, and while this succeeded in making me feel guilty, somewhere inside me, even at the age of four, there was a strong certainty that God could not be like that. Jesus definitely wasn't, as he refused to stone the adulterous woman, and kept saying, "Your sins are forgiven." But in one way or another, God was an incontrovertible part of life.

So I got a shock when, at the age of twelve, at school assembly, a university student was invited to come and talk about the views of Sartre and Albert Camus and their philosophy of The Absurd: God did not exist, it was just a comforting, man-made illusion, and life had no meaning. I was stunned. I had had no idea that there were people who did not believe in God. And of course these philosophers stated that it was cowardice that prevented one from facing the true facts.

That evening I lay in bed, my world in tatters. I was a stickler for truth, and if what these people said was true, then I could not ignore it. On the other hand, God was what gave meaning and purpose to life, and if life had no meaning, I didn't see how I could live. Finally two things came to mind to save me. I had a great love of nature, and I suddenly thought of the beauty of sunsets—surely as long as sunsets existed, life could not be without meaning. This satisfied my intuitive self. Then a more rational argument also came to help me. It went like this: the existence of God cannot be proved. But then neither can anyone prove that God does not exist. So if there is no proof one way or the other, I am free to choose and cannot be accused of running away from the truth. So I can choose that God does exist. This thought brought great relief, and I went to sleep peacefully.

As I grew up, I began to have problems with the beliefs of the Christian church, and I got stuck with the feeling that I had to accept the whole package or sink back into a materialist, godless view of life, which was for me unthinkable. So I tried to make myself believe, went to church, tried to 'practise' my religion, all the time feeling a fraud, and untrue to myself. I met a pastor who preached in a natural, unpretentious way, and I went to see him with great hopes of finding a sympathetic response to my main question: how come Jesus could be seen as the only son of God, and the other religions just taken as 'nice stories.' Having read that Krishna also had a resurrection story, it struck me that if I had been born a Hindu, this would feel real to me, and Jesus would be 'a nice story.' This did not make sense, and it also felt unworthy of God, to come just once in one part of the world: if He was all wise and powerful, how could he choose to be so uneconomical? Alas, the pastor totally disappointed me by simply repeating that Jesus was unique and drawing on historical sources to lend proof to it, etc, etc. It was then that I felt I must give up on the church and find my own way.

The year before I was to meet Baba, I was at a seminar at the University of York, which had beautiful grounds; I walked there among huge trees and discovered an old red brick house with this motto: "God Shows Himself in All Things." This was a nice confirmation of my new philosophy that I could find God in trees and starry skies. I also had an epiphany moment, suddenly seeing that just as all things were ordered like a beautiful symphony in the physical world, the planets following their course according to immutable laws, similarly, this was true of everything that happened, every detail of life was part of a pattern, though it was so much more complex that we could not see it and it seemed chaotic. But the profound intuition was that NOTHING WAS OUT OF TUNE— every single event was part of the symphony. This was a powerful moment and the insight remained with me and supported me in the following ups and downs of life.

I feel that all these steps on my journey were preparing me for the arrival of Baba as the last piece that made sense of the whole puzzle; this, I believe, was why I could accept him so totally and immediately. To be told that God came again and again with different names in different parts of the world; that all religions were after the same truth and none was better than another; that God was forgiving and approachable and was everywhere and in everything, that Baba and Jesus were one and the same: this brought such peace. It was a confirmation of everything I had thought but not found any agreement within the outside world. I went back to reading the Gospels from beginning to end, and felt strongly, "This is the same voice, it has the same authority of One who knows and speaks the truth."

So the start of my journey with Baba was founded on Truth. My encounter was not about falling in love, as other people have described. I felt honestly that I could not pretend to love someone I had not met in the flesh. I didn't like the term 'Baba lover,' and I thought the most I could say about myself was that I was 'a follower.'

However this story is called "A Tale of Finding Love," so how did I get there? I had always seen myself as a seeker of truth, and Baba progressively answered all my questions, met all the needs of my mind. I absorbed *God Speaks* eagerly, not understanding much of it, but exhilarated by the idea that "this was the story of creation, by someone who was there!" I could trust Baba's teachings totally, and this calmed my questioning mind. Reading the *Discourses*, after the initial resistance to Eastern concepts (sanskara*s*, maya and the like), I was particularly struck by Baba's acute understanding of psychology, being a trained psychotherapist myself. Reincarnation was no problem, and it seemed to make sense of apparently unfair lives. So I was quite happy to continue to find my way into Baba's teachings, to increase my understanding, and I didn't feel the need to fall in love.

Then Baba got me to come to India. Quite against my will, as I was reluctant to meet disciples who might not be as open and tolerant to other religions as Baba was, and I resisted the trend of Western people pursuing Eastern beliefs. But things took their own course—Baba seemed to arrange it all, even finding me a travelling companion. I remember talking to Baba's picture and saying, "But Baba, I don't want to go to India!" Baba replied, "I know you don't, but you are going!"

So in December 1980, I found myself on a plane to Bombay. The journey was as difficult as it could be: the plane was late, we got into a pirate taxi, missed our train, got on the wrong train, waited for ages for a train to Poona in a God-forsaken station and my companion, whom I supposed to be level-headed because she had a PhD, threw a tantrum saying she was not spiritual enough to go on a pilgrimage, and threatened to get on a train which said "Bangalore" just to get out of this station! We were too late to get to Ahmednagar that day and had to spend a night in Poona on the floor of a room occupied by my sister who was visiting the Rajneesh ashram. During the night as the hard floor prevented sleep, I was thinking negative thoughts about Rajneesh, his ashram and the behaviour of his 'disciples,' when Baba clearly said to me, "Don't make differences; it is all My work."

So there were plenty of obstacles to overcome until we finally found our way to the Samadhi, where the shocks continued. I had imagined Baba's tomb as a huge beautiful building a bit like the

Taj Mahal, and there was this small, unassuming structure. "Of course," I suddenly thought, "this is Bethlehem!" Worse, I didn't like the photo of Baba inside it, nor the paintings on the walls, and I hated the plastic flowers in garish vases which were around in those days. I sat there feeling completely out of place, when I suddenly noticed that the wooden battens of the closed window behind Baba's picture made the shape of a cross. Relief! Perhaps there was something here for me after all. Finally I stepped out of the Tomb and went to sit beside it under a tree, with the beautifully spacious view of India spread at my feet. I said to Baba, "Why did I have to come all this way?" The reply came, "You had to come all this way in order to know that you *don't* have to come all this way." That made sense.

It was not until my first visit to Meherazad that my heart was touched. Suspicious of 'disciples' and fearing they might be evangelical, I went in a defiant mood, wearing a very visible Celtic cross around my neck. The first response I got was Mani exclaiming: "What a beautiful cross! Where did you get it?" The next thing was Eruch wearing a teeshirt saying "Assisi" in large letters. And, as happens in Mandali Hall, while I was sitting there quietly feeling shy, someone mentioned her conflict of loyalties between Jesus and Baba.

Eruch replied, "Well, if you are drawn to Christ, be drawn to Christ. It is all the same thing." I had my answer.

I felt so accepted and welcomed by all. Bal Natu, hearing my name, Aude, said, "I have an Ode for you!" and hurrying back to his little room, he returned with a piece of paper on which he had written the following: "The wine of God's grace has no brim; if it appears to have a brim, tis the fault of the cup!" "This is by Rumi, an Ode for you," he repeated.

The warm, unconditional love radiated by the mandali, their humour, ordinariness and lack of judgement opened me up like a flower in the sun, and all my defences started crumbling. Soon I was sitting on Mehera's porch, listening to a song about "the fires of separation" and weeping as if my heart would break. The floodgates had opened, the love story had begun.

I thought I had arrived, but of course it was only the beginning of the journey, and I had no idea what Baba would take me through, after the initial honeymoon: the painful stripping of cherished ideas and attachments, old habits, the mental anguish of mistaken relationships, the hard experience of physical illness and diminishing capacities. How many times I was reminded of Mani's tale about the potter, who with one hand bangs the clay into shape with a hammer, whilst the other hand, invisible inside the pot, supports it and keeps if from breaking. Through all the trials I held on to Baba's presence, and the intimacy and closeness grew. Increasingly I felt love for him, having grown acquainted with his human side through the stories of his life, and learning a great deal about how he trained his disciples and close ones.

But it took a long time to be able to accept the fact that God loved me. (*Me?* This mess of contradictions, unruly emotions, weaknesses and failures? Why should he bother?) However, after a journey of nearly forty years, I am now able to look into Baba's eyes and know that I am loved, and that the love I feel for him is nothing else but the reflection of his love for me. Receiving this Love is now the focus of my days, along with remembrance and trying to please him. My only prayer is one of gratitude for his countless blessings, the greatest being his daily companionship, and the extraordinary good fortune of knowing that God has come again in human form, to help us all to free ourselves from illusion and wake up to Reality.

*****

Now I live in Norwich, a cathedral city in England. I have lived there since 1979, having moved from my home country, Switzerland. After some years as a psychotherapist, in 1990 I founded the King of Hearts for People and the Arts, an Arts centre with exhibitions, concerts and story-telling, named after Meher Baba of course. The centre closed in 2010 due to lack of funds so I am now retired, with much time on my hands to spend with Baba and respond to whatever he sends me. I still run three or four concerts of Baroque music a year in a local eighteenth century chapel. I am a wife, mother, mother-in-law, step-mother and grandmother.

Jai Meher Baba. Thanks Be to God.

101 Tales of Finding Love

FINDING MY WAY TO BABA

by Hugh Huntington

Artwork © Claire Mataira

y journey to find Baba, I now know, began in childhood. My family had a lineage of Baptist and Presbyterian ministers going back several generations. The Baptist church my parents joined when I was three years old was founded on the principle of education of children. The approach was non-traditional in that we were encouraged to think, laughable as that may be for a child, rather than emphasizing the dogma of sin and guilt through failure. A dichotomy erupted in my mind birthed by the split of the church's approach to God and Jesus and the guilt, shame and sin messages that my parents' lineage conveyed emotionally—or in fairness to them, what I absorbed.

We did not experience pressure to join or conform as the church emphasized the individual's relationship to God rather than conformity and compliance in the name of religion. Little did I know then of the importance of this foundation.

When I was a teenager a new minister, Carlisle Marney, came to the church. Raised in the backwoods of east Tennessee, he emerged into the life of the Myers Park Baptist church as a powerful theologian who rattled the timbers of conventional spiritual expression. The first real ego differentiation between my parents and myself appeared one spring Sunday morning when, as we left the church, my parents griped about "not understanding a word he said," whereas my experience of that sermon was an energetic resonance with a truth that was beyond my ability to articulate. He laid the foundation in me of being responsible for my relationship with God and kindled a deep longing to know who this man Jesus was beyond the classical trappings of organized Christian religion.

By the time I returned to Charlotte, North Carolina after five years of college and four years of Air Force duty, Carlisle Marney had been forced to retire due to a failing heart. I made a brief and final connection with him at Lake Junaluska where he had established a counseling program for ministers who had burned out on religion. By this time I had begun the journey of self-exploration through an attempt to understand energetic manifestations of how we humans express and experience ourselves beyond the world of the intellect and materialism. These explorations included past life experiences, psychic phenomenon, Kirlian photography, healing the body through the manifestation of chi or qi (oriental teachings), explorations of my roots in Mayan culture and Christian monasteries, Chinese philosophy through the study of Taoism and Tai Chi/Chi Gong, a short stint as a member of the Vestry of an Episcopal church, years of participation in personal growth workshops, and the experience of studying Native American spirituality with a Lakota Medicine man for many years.

Taoism studied through the *I Ching* or *Book of Change* can be used as a divination tool, of which Baba did not approve. My teacher taught it from the standpoint of understanding how change occurs, which is not well understood in Western culture. In hindsight I realize that it has given me a broader understanding of forces in nature that, without being conscious of those forces, have predictable behavioral expressions. I link these to Baba's teaching about sanskaras. An example is an understanding that emotions are part of our given nature. However, when we allow the emotions to become elevated such as excitement, we will experience the cyclical downswing of depression or bad moods. The same is true in reverse.

While studying to become a shaman in the Lakota tradition, I experienced many energies beyond traditional western beliefs, but most important I learned about how ego shows up in spiritual or religious practice. Two lessons stand out. First, there is an element of passion in spirituality, but spirituality is not passion. Second, there is a place for ritual in spiritual growth but ritual (through ego demands) becomes dogma and dogma always turns dark or evil. Baba has taught us to not make of him a religion. Avoiding the overuse of ritual is critical to fulfill that instruction. In all these journeys I never lost the deep sense of connection with Jesus and became clearer about who he was as a man and how his message has been distorted by organized religion.

Hugh Huntington

During the final years of living in Taos, New Mexico, I first learned of Meher Baba. Only after I moved to western North Carolina did I begin the exploration into his meaning in my life. On my first trip to the Meher Spiritual Center in 1999 the librarian suggested that I read the *Discourses*. Never in all my various wanderings had I found any writing, theory or any one that so clearly understood the relationship between ego and mankind's behavioral expression—his language is sanskaras; my root origin word was sin. The *Discourses* offered me greater clarity about how to be responsible for my behavior and how to be aware of the origins/roots of those behaviors deep in my being.

For the last twelve years I have become intensely interested in the teaching of James Tolchard (now deceased) and the writing of Dr. David Hawkins and his understanding of the primary emotions (seen as trances) by which we live our typical day and the relationship of those emotions to our behaviors and our health. Baba's teaching about the ego has helped me learn to release unhealthy emotions expressed though the trance of the moment and move to more positive emotions. I believe that this helps me to wear out old sanskaras and limit the creation of new sanskaras.

I believe that Baba guided me through all of my wanderings because new opportunities continuously presented themselves, many of which I chose to explore. I feel blessed to have found my way to Baba again, having only recently realized that I first knew and loved Baba in the man named Jesus.

*****

I currently live near Marshall, North Carolina on a twenty-five-acre farm, but will be moving into Asheville when a new owner is found. My consulting practice in organizational behavior closed in 2015. I recently invested in rental property which my oldest daughter and I manage together. I am involved with four other people currently establishing and learning to operate Meher Archive Collective. This is wonderful work finding, digitizing and collecting artifacts from the life of Avatar Meher Baba.

101 Tales of Finding Love

MEHER BABA MAKES HIS POINT

by Donnalyn Karpeles

Donnalyn at Arthur's Seat, Mahabaleshwar, 1973.
This structure fell off the cliff a year or so later.

In the summer of 1972, I was twenty-three years old and an American student living in France. I was a hippie like many young people then and still used drugs like marijuana and hashish. One day, I made cookies with hashish in them and after eating some I had a very realistic experience. I experienced being born, living, dying and then being reborn. How this was portrayed was me riding on a rollercoaster. I would be in my mother's womb as the rollercoaster slowly went up the first hill. At the top, I was born and my life was a fast ride of ups and downs until death when the rollercoaster stopped. Then I was on the ride again and again. I lost count after thirty-six times or lifetimes. I had always believed in reincarnation and this vision seemed to 'prove' that reincarnation was true, but I didn't know if it was or it was induced by the hashish. So I said to myself, "The next experience I have must be real and not while using drugs." So I never took drugs again.

Then Janet, my best girlfriend from high school, came to travel in Europe and we decided to go to India together. Her father was a Lutheran minister and was in charge of all the Lutheran missionaries in South East Asia. Her dream was to go and visit India where her father was born when his parents were missionaries there.

After much preparation with vaccinations and other things, we were finally able to start out at the end of November. We hitch-hiked through Europe, but once we got to Turkey, we decided it would be safer to take buses and trains. This was a time when many young people were traveling to India overland. It was a great adventure for everyone.

We got to a Turkish city before Iran and met up with two German boys named Wolfgang and Wolfgang. We asked if we could travel with them thinking that would be extra protection. Unfortunately, they were drug-using hippies and very unreliable and irresponsible. One of them even got left behind at the Iranian border while his friend slept on the bus. Luckily Janet noticed it and we were able stop for him as he raced to the bus in a taxi.

In Teheran, we met two Dutch boys from Amsterdam who were going to Nagpur, India for a three-month study of water purification as part of their university degree. They both were tall, blond, very upstanding and never used drugs. We asked if we could travel with them instead of the German boys. Since they had some time to travel, they wanted to head south to a town called Esfahan and then go through the desert and up to Pakistan instead of going through Afghanistan which is how everyone else was going because that was the drug route. We got to Esfahan and it seemed we were the only foreigners there. Walking through the city, we did see an American couple so we started talking to them.

The wife was wearing a necklace with the picture of a man on it. When I saw it, I thought it was the ugliest thing I had ever seen and couldn't imagine why anyone would wear such a necklace.

I asked who he was and she said "Meher Baba, our spiritual master" and that they were going to where he had lived in India. I was interested to hear more, since I had loved Jesus and God until I was fourteen, at which time I was unconvinced God existed. Inwardly, I wanted to believe in God, but had no proof that He could be real.

"So you are going to see this Meher Baba?"

"No, He died in 1969."

"Well, are you going there to meditate?"

"No, there is no meditation. We sit and listen to His disciples tell stories about His life and also, He didn't speak for forty-four years." Well, this was too much for me. Meher Baba was dead, there was no meditation, He didn't talk and He was very unattractive. I had no further interest although to be polite, I did read a little booklet about Him that they gave me to read.

To continue our journey, we had to travel eight hours by bus to a small city called Zahedan and sleep out in the desert and wait for the early morning milk train to take us to Quetta and then Lahore. It was a long trip of two days but when we got to Lahore, which is on the border with India we found out that because of the Indio-Pakistani War going on, the border was only open on Fridays. We arrived Friday evening, so we had to spend a week in Lahore. Since we were now all friends, the six of us shared one big hotel room. On Christmas morning, we woke up and found little presents at the foot of our beds. The American couple had gotten up early, gone to the market and bought us presents. We and the Dutch boys went out and got everyone presents too, and celebrated together. So, even though, I was not attracted to Meher Baba, I really liked these American followers of His.

Friday came and we crossed the border into India. The Dutch boys went to Nagpur, we went to Delhi to stay with a missionary family and the couple went on to Ahmednagar, the city near Meherazad and Meherabad, Meher Baba's home and tomb.

After a week, Janet and I set off on our travels planning to go to the beach city of Goa but stopping off to see the Ajanta and Ellora caves. The Ellora caves are near Aurangabad, which is a short distance to Ahmednagar. Janet said that she wanted to go there to see where the couple had told us they would be. I had a strong negative feeling and said I didn't want to go, but she insisted, so we got on a bus and went. We got to the bus station and she showed people the address she had and we walked a few miles followed by school children who kept screaming "Jai Baba, Jai Baba" at us. I had heard of Meher Baba, but I didn't know who "Jay Baba" was.

We found where we were going and were shown to a hotel where a lot of Westerners were staying. Then a very nice Indian woman came over to us and tried to give me a hug saying "Jai Baba." I pushed her away and said we were not there for Meher Baba, but were there to see our friends. She put us in a horse-drawn carriage and told the driver to take us to Meherabad where Meher Baba's tomb is located and where our friends would be. That very nice woman was Dr. Goher, who had been with Meher Baba since the 1940s.

We walked up the hill and there they were. They showed us around and I decided that this was another tourist attraction and treated it as such. We visited the museum and saw Meher Baba's bicycle, sandals, coats and other things. We met Mansari, the tiny woman who had lived alone on the hill for thirty years even before Meher Baba was buried there. And then they showed us the tomb itself. I saw people go in and bow down and decided I would never go in because there was no way that I could ever bow down to something I didn't believe in.

We learned out friends were going to stay a few more days before going to Bombay to take the boat that went to Goa, although they would get off sooner at a beach called Ratnagiri. It made sense to all travel together again and we were told that they didn't want to leave until Friday afternoon because Friday morning was when the women disciples would come to say prayers at the tomb. I thought this would be another tourist thing to do, so we were there Friday morning, too.

Nowadays, when prayers are said, everyone stands outside the tomb, but then people could say them inside and on the days when the women disciples came, only women could go inside. To this day, I do not know how it happened, but somehow I was pushed inside and not just inside, but up to the far right side in the corner. The tomb was filled with women and I was trapped with no escape. While the prayers were being said, all I could think of was, "How am I going to get out of here without bowing down? I don't want to offend anyone, but I can't bow down." While standing there and thinking this, I would look around the tomb and my eyes kept resting on a woman standing in the opposite corner. Even though she was in her fifties I thought she was the most beautiful woman I had ever seen. I couldn't stop looking at her. I don't think she ever looked at me because she was so engrossed in saying the prayers and looking lovingly at Meher Baba's photo. I didn't know it at the time, but this was Mehera, Meher Baba's chief woman disciple, who Meher Baba said was the only person who loved Him as He should be loved.

All of a sudden I felt a bolt of electricity go through the top of my head through my body and out my fingers and toes. I started crying. I felt so embarrassed that I forced myself to stop the tears, but then my nose started to run and run, and all I could do was stand there wiping my nose on my arms which was even more embarrassing than crying. My mind was a complete blank and then my very first thought was, "Well, of course, you can bow down." And that was the first time of many times that I did bow down to Him.

We later left and it was decided that we would go all together to Ratnagiri for a week and then go back to Ahmednagar at the end of the month for the Amartithi celebration of when Meher Baba dropped his physical form to live in His Lovers' hearts forever. I remember being in total bliss and not eating or sleeping very much. I thought this is how all Meher Baba followers felt and was convinced that I would be in that state for the rest of my life. On the fifth day at the beach, I was watching the little crabs run up and down the sand when I remembered what I had said five months earlier. I had said that I wanted my next experience to be real and not because of drugs. I realized that I had just had the most real experience of my life with no drugs. I looked up at the sky and I said, "Baba, you've made your point, I understand," and then within half an hour my wonderful blissful state slowly deflated like a leaky balloon and I was back to normal.

And this is how I came to Meher Baba. It is the most important thing that has ever happened to me and I am eternally grateful that He has been with me all these years.

*****

Donnalyn Karpeles has been living in Santa Barbara, California for thirty-six years. After following advice from Mani and listening inwardly to Meher Baba, she went into the ego-crushing Real Estate profession, holding on to His damaan through all life's twists and turns.

Avatar Meher Baba Ki Jai!!

101 Tales of Finding Love

MY BIOGRAPHY, CONTACT & ACTIVITIES

by Birendra Kumar

Meher Baba 1954

Release of Birendra Kumar's book titles at
Meher Baba Delhi Centre February 12, 2016

I originally belonged to a town named Chunar in the Mirzapur District of Utter Pradesh. I did my schooling in Chunar. I came to Varanasi and passed the intermediate and Degree in Electrical Engineering from BHU in 1968. For a year in 1969 I worked with the Private Supply Company in Firozabad and Shikohabad (both In Uttar Pradesh) as a Trainee Engineer. Thereafter, I came to Delhi in 1970, served in CPWD for six years and ITDC for twenty-eight years. I took voluntary retirement in 2004 at the age of fifty-six. Thereafter I have engaged myself in freelance consultancy for Electrical works which is computer based. I am now over sixty-nine years and well settled in Delhi with my family by Baba's grace.

I came to know about Meher Baba long ago through my father who came to Delhi in 1957 for temporary service after retrenchment from Central ordinance Depot Allahabad. He came to know about Baba through his office employee, Sri Kishan Lal Bhasin. My father had the opportunity to have Baba's darshan in Poona in 1964.

In 1967, while I was in a hostel in Varanasi, I had a lot of mental worry and Baba appeared in my dream and said, *Come to me, I will help you.* When I came to Delhi in 1970, I recollected my dream and had the intuition to read Baba's literature. I read *God Speaks, Listen, Humanity, The Everything and Nothing,* etc. I had the darshan of Balyogeashwarji, Sathya Sai Baba but had no effect of their godliness. By that time, Baba had dropped His body. On an intellectual reading of Baba's philosophy and His declarations, I inferred, rather Baba made me to infer, that in the contemporary period, if there is any possibility of any Avatarhood it can be only Meher Baba. It is very difficult to accept or even conceptualize the whole world as a dream. I don't know to what extent I accept Baba as Avatar, but when I speak to someone I always say that Baba is the Avatar. He is to be taken only as the Avatar and not as a saint or sadhu, as declared by Baba.

Baba's revelation on the theme of creation in *God Speaks* and His directives in simple words to remember Him constantly and wholeheartedly the best way as you can is the gist of His teaching for the safest, surest and quickest way to reach God. It most appealed to me. I am convinced that there can be no better way to explain the gist of spiritual philosophy. Baba said, "Spiritual literature of the Avatar or a Sadguru is worth reading and real food for thought." Exactly, when I read any other spiritual literature of a sect or saint other than Meher Baba, I feel it of a much lower standard compared to Baba's philosophy and find no interest in reading it. According to me, Baba has made such a difficult goal of realisation so easy for us.

One more fact which I have experienced many times is that Meher Baba has made me to realise that He is supreme and His will pervades above everything. Any assignment undertaken by me, however carefully undertaken, will not be perfect, but it will have some shortcoming in my work. Every time I feel that particular thing could have been done in a better way, but I failed, as it was not Baba's will.

In 1971, I had the intuition to translate *God Speaks* into Hindi. I translated about one hundred and fifty pages of *God Speaks*. My father suggested that I send the translated manuscript to Secretary Adi K. Irani and get his opinion about whether the translation was up to the mark and true to its meaning. I sent the manuscript to Adi K. Irani. He appreciated my effort, as it amounts to a kind of meditation, and wrote that a Hindi translation of *God Speaks* had already been undertaken by Sri Keshav Narayan Nigam of Hamirpur. Hence thereafter I discontinued my translation.

I don't remember the year, once more I dreamed that Meher Baba had come to my house and I was introducing all my family members to Meher Baba in English.

Beginning in 1971, very often, I used to attend weekly Baba's *Satsang*/gatherings along with my father at the residence of Sh. W.D. Kain in President Estate (Delhi) on Sundays and at the residence of Dr. Hukumat Rai Kapil in Sarojini Nagar (Delhi) on Fridays.

In my service from 1981 to 1992, I was posted at different places viz: Udaipur, Puri, Varanasi and Delhi. My father died in May 1985. After my posting in Delhi since 1992, I was associated with activities of the Delhi Centre. Earlier, there was no building of an Avatar Meher Baba Centre in Delhi. Its registered address in Delhi was the residence of Sardar Mohkam Singh (H/o Smt. Kusum Singh) B-171, Greater Kailash -1 New Delhi 48. Annual functions used to be held in a rented hall. In 1989, the foundation stone for the construction of a centre's building was laid at Tuglakabad by Alobaji on land purchased from Delhi Development Authority.

Construction of the centre's building was undertaken in 1991-1992. Being an engineer, I was associated with construction of this building from very beginning as member of construction committee. I carried out the supervision of works (civil, electrical, plumbing and sanitary etc) including procurement of materials and finishing work at labour rates to save on cost.

After my voluntary retirement in 2004, time passed but suddenly in 2013 I had the intuition to compile humorous episodes of Meher Baba from *Lord Meher* and other books by His close disciples and published two volumes in 2014. Thereafter Baba made me an instrument to compile five more books, which are as follows:

1. *Lessons for Spiritual Aspirants*—Eighty topics on spirituality, released in January 2015.

2. *Semblance Episodes*—Fifty-two episodes of Baba compared with mythological episodes, released in August, 2016.

3. *Articles*—Eighty-seven articles on different topics based on Baba's discourses, released in November, 2016.

4. *Stories and Similes by Meher Baba & His Close Disciples*—One hundred and thirty-six stories, likely to be released in March 2017.

5. *Fortunate Souls* —Past and present souls who met Meher Baba in seventeen groups with state wide list and about one thousand biographies—compilation already undertaken and likely to be published in parts in 2017 onward. This is going to be an authentic record to be kept in AMB libraries.

Avatar Meher Baba Prasar Kendra, Delhi, having its office of correspondence at B-2/62 sector-16, Delhi-110089, was incorporated on 22-11-2015. Its objective—activities, Baba's messages, stories, episodes, philosophy and information can be read on the exclusive website www.ambprasarkendra.com on Meher Baba launched on Amartithi 2016.

Birendra Kumar
B-2/62, Sector-16, Rohini, Delhi 110089
Mob: 09711789177
E-mail ID: meherbk@gmail.com

101 Tales of Finding Love

From Darkness to Light

by Raymond Lee

Meher Baba, 1957

Ray at the pool at Pilgrim
Pines, L.A. Sahavas some
time in the 1970s

I have come to sow the seed of love in your hearts.

— Meher Baba

On an elementary school field trip to Griffith Park Observatory in Los Angeles, I find myself in a queue outside with my fellow students, walking toward the main building when, for a moment, I become aware of something—an aspect of existence—vaguely discerned, undefined but definitely present. A year or two later wandering through an empty schoolyard on a vacant Sunday afternoon, a window opened and I became aware of something existing alongside the everyday reality I had become habituated to. I was unaware that anyone else was having any kind of similar experience. So, if I was the only one who felt something radically different, was it real or was it my imagination? One day, in Catholic elementary school we were studying the Old Testament and we came across the story of Jacob's ladder. With a flash of understanding, I intuitively recognized the image as the mystical path ascending to God.

By at least age ten I had become aware of a profound sense of shame, unworthiness and alienation. As a kid, I had a tenuous grip on self-esteem. At the same time, my mother whose grip on sanity had never been that strong was going over the edge into full-blown psychosis and began exhibiting symptoms of paranoid schizophrenia. She became a high volume screamer and fully believed what her fevered imagination told her—that my sister and I were daily conniving ways to torment her. I knew there was something wrong with her, but the silence from my father about her condition promoted the belief that there was also something wrong with me. For nearly the rest of her life, she was medicated with a mix of strong anti-psychotics and uppers and downers. Through the miracle of modern chemistry she was kept at home and out of mental institutions, but her condition and the drugs limited her available empathy. My father, like many men of the post-war era, was generally emotionally absent although beneath the surface, I felt the vast chasm of estrangement between the two of us, as well as his unspoken hatred for me.

As a child I came to believe the world was a hostile place and I had long since decided the safest way to live was in my head only since feelings, like parents, were not to be trusted. I remained as small/quiet/invisible as possible so that I might survive. All my effort went to reading other people in order to appear non-threatening and compliant. In the deepest part of me my own sanity was up for grabs. The tremendous effort to appear normal superseded all other endeavors and was a full time 24/7/365 occupation. I had very few resources left over. Consequently, I was barely a "C" student, had trouble concentrating and could not always complete homework assignments, although I would occasionally test well above expectations.

Those early childhood momentary awarenesses of something were long forgotten by the time I arrived at college in northern California in early September 1968. A few weeks into the semester, I was lying on my dorm room bed alone at dusk as I became aware of a presence. A whitish figure appeared and, as I watched spellbound, approached. Now beside me, the figure reached down and, slowly extending its hand, touched my heart. The very next instant the apparition vanished. What just happened?!? What was that? All I could think of was that somehow it was Jesus. That was a natural thought as I had grown up immersed in Catholicism—had become an altar boy, attended a Catholic elementary school, high school and was now enrolled at a Catholic College.

2. GERMINATION:

As the next day dawned and I walked through campus on my way to class, an unsettling sense grew stronger by the minute. Something inside me had shifted. With mounting horror, I realized that EVERYTHING had shifted. Something was different. I didn't know what it was but whatever it was, my psyche was being upended and the fragile mental balance I had maintained had collapsed. I struggled in vain to locate my old survival strategy. Instead, I found myself naked and vulnerable in a perceived hostile world. I could no longer manage life in the way I was used to. I could not hide behind a facade of normalcy. The desperation that had lurked beneath the surface was in full view and there was no shoving it back underground. Having recourse to no other solution, I tried harder than ever to appear OK.

It didn't work. I began to miss classes. Panic dogged me wherever I went. Whatever ability I had to study was now completely gone. At home for the holidays, I told my parents I couldn't continue at school. They wanted to know why. I could not say. How do you say, "Jesus came into my room, touched my heart and I'm now in constant inner turmoil"? I could not tell anyone what I experienced as I was certain that I would be judged insane—and my worst nightmare would come to pass. I would have to admit I was irredeemably broken.

My parents arranged a meeting with my old high school vice principal. Maybe he could get to the bottom of this and straighten me out. Talking with us, he decided I was freaked out by being in unfamiliar circumstances away from home. Not an uncommon reaction, he said. Typical anxiety for a more sensitive than most young person; but the best thing was to return to college after the break. He was sure I would hit my stride and everything would be fine.

I returned to school—everything was not fine. Where before I managed to attend a class now and then, after the break it was completely beyond me to show up for any classes at all. The end of the semester saw me leave that school for good.

Returning home, I enrolled in the local community college. Being home and having a routine did help. Familiar circumstances also helped. I was able to make a couple of friends at college who introduced me to psychedelics. Under the influence of LSD I began to understand 'the cosmic big picture' and figure out big things about the meaning of life and once or twice I experienced sub-subtle visuals. But my drug-induced insights were always temporary. I could never bring those realizations back into ordinary life—they would always evaporate as I came down and try as I might I could never regain the glimpses of transcendence. After a year and a half, the camaraderie of the drug brotherhood wore thin and I found myself isolated and frightened once again. I more or less stopped getting high. Although the distraction of drugs was fleeting, the momentary acid flashbacks would come and go for years thereafter. Those insights and occult experiences had been helpful in confirming that there was more to life than meets the eye, but the psychedelics were not helpful with what I needed most—integration of my head and heart. I was a splintered person before the drugs and even more so afterwards.

I experienced an undercurrent of anxiety coupled with desperation and there seemed no escape from this untenable situation. At the crossroads of despair and desperation, I was compelled to seek a way out. Over the course of the following year, I picked up *The Egyptian Book of the Dead*, the *Quran* and the *Bhagavad Gita*. I could make no sense of any of it but I was compelled to seek relief.

Graduating from junior college, I then enrolled at California State University, Los Angeles for the fall semester. In late August my parents departed on a three-month trip to the East Coast. They promised to check in on me by phone every once in a while. The first two or three weeks of the fall semester, I managed to attend classes at my new school. But before long an overwhelming terror seized me. I would be walking across campus on the way to my next class and as I walked I would notice a fellow student look up as we crossed paths. Imagining they could see into me, I shuddered at the thought that they knew I was not right. I imagined they could look into my soul and see that I was broken. I believed I was utterly transparent to everyone. That's when I heard John Lennon's song *Crippled Inside*: "One thing you can't hide, is when you're crippled inside."

Over the course of the next week or two, I stopped going to class. I was too haunted by terror and so retreated into the safety of my room. When my parents would call, I would put them off with assurances that everything was fine. One time a friend stopped by to say hello, but the moment was so awkward and I was so full of fear—I was so transparently 'not right'—that he soon departed and never returned. My fear of others was paralyzing, the self-loathing was incapacitating and my general depression and anxiety was sapping my will to live. The most I could muster was to furtively venture out every two or three weeks to the grocery store. I began to sleep upwards of eighteen hours a day. Being awake was torture.

3. Pushing toward the Light:

Eventually my parents returned and there was a big scene. My mother took the position that my not going to school was another scheme to torture her. In her paranoid mind, I was doing this 'to' her. I had been trying to get at her and had come up with this unique way—becoming anxious and depressed to the point of catatonia— all intended to make her suffer.

Our family doctor recommended a psychiatrist colleague. In our weekly sessions I began to appreciate the sympathetic ear of this good man. He would listen to me rage on about my impossible parents—for I had come to blame them for my condition. After all, I had grown up with criticism, hostility, fear, ridicule and shame. The doctor diagnosed me as having an anxiety disorder. He prescribed a strong anxiety relieving sedative popular in the day. In the course of a couple of weeks, I finished the first bottle of pills. My anxiety may have been temporarily relieved, but it didn't take long for the hound of hell to catch up with me.

One evening while waiting for my appointment time to roll around, I was parked in a secluded spot overlooking downtown Los Angeles. Convinced that I was doomed to pointless and endless torment, I decided to take my own life. I downed an entire fresh bottle of pills and drove to the appointment. Afterward I had dinner at a local greasy spoon and then went home to bed.

Waking up the next day, I was fine. It was several years before I remembered the incident.

I got a job in the mailroom of an insurance company. It got me out of the house, gave me a little spending money, provided some interaction with others and gave me some stability. At night I would listen to an underground FM radio station broadcasting out of the basement of a nearby church. I would listen to talks by Alan Watts and others. One night I heard a talk by Baba Ram Dass. He was talking about his new book, *Be Here Now*. Something deep inside resonated to his words. I bought a copy of his book and devoured it like a starving man. Somewhere in the middle of the book I noticed a woodcut representation of someone called Meher Baba.

My old drug friends from junior college called up. They were going to be driving down to a Grateful Dead concert in San Diego. Did I want to go? On the way south, we each took a blotter square of LSD. Before it kicked in, I asked about the guy in the book, Meher Baba. My friends didn't know much about him, but one of them said there was a bookstore in Pasadena dedicated to him. They gave me the address—31 East Union Street.

Weeks passed into summer. One day, I remembered about the Meher Baba Bookstore. The address my friends had given me was about five miles away. It was a hot summer Sunday afternoon and I borrowed my dad's car. In the early 1970s the old section of Pasadena that dated back to the 1850s was still a skid row. The drunks and the crazies lived on the narrow streets, alleyways and parks. Parking on the vacant street, I got out and looked for the address. The block had nothing but boarded up stores and broken windows. Derelict two-story brick buildings from another era lined both sides of the street. Not finding the number on the south side of the street, I crossed to the north side. Nope. No 31 East Union. Disappointed, I drove home. Weeks passed. On another hot summer Sunday afternoon later in the summer, I again remembered the Meher Baba Bookstore. Maybe I hadn't searched the street thoroughly enough and had somehow overlooked the place. The feeling was insistent—I had to get there! Borrowing my dad's car, I again drove back to the same block. It was deserted as before. As diligently as I could, I searched both sides of the street. It was difficult to concentrate and remain focused, but again there was no 31 East Union. Dejected, I drove home.

Weeks passed. It was now Labor Day weekend. I suddenly remembered the Meher Baba Bookstore. I MUST find it! With an insistence that crowded out every other thought, for the third time I drove up to East Union Street. Determined to find it, I took my time and really looked at each and every inch of wall, door and brick on both sides of the street. Twice. It still wasn't there. Despairing, I conceded defeat and was about to get back into the car, when the thought came—maybe my friend meant 31 WEST Union. I looked up at the nearby street sign. Fair Oaks Avenue is the dividing line in Pasadena for streets that go East-West. I walked across Fair Oaks to the west side of Union. There it was! The Meher Baba Bookstore! 31 WEST Union Street. It had been there the whole time! It was closed but the store hours were on the door and there was a poster in the window advertising a "MEHER BABA LOVE IN" happening that very day up in Berkeley. That's why they were closed—everyone must be at the Love In. But, the bookstore would be open the following Thursday night.

4. THE SUNSHINE OF THE SPIRIT:

As I read my first Baba books, *The Secret of Sleep* and *The Advancing Stream of Life*, I was hit by the sense that here at last was the truth. Finally I had come across the real deal, the Truth, and it was being explained in a way I could grasp. I felt the resonance of certainty deep within. I got ahold of *God Speaks* and devoured it over a weekend of non-stop reading. My roommate from my first college was in town and I turned him on to Meher Baba. Comparing notes after some serious book study, he believed he was on the six plane, whereas I took a more humble approach and considered myself to be no more than a fifth planer.

I began to attend Friday night meetings at the Meher Baba Bookstore. One exceptionally hot night, Darwin and Jean Shaw were there. Darwin spoke of Baba as the Christ with a certainty beyond faith. His talk warmed my soul. This was something real. I felt a relief and a peace I had never known.

I read Baba's admonition about drugs. Much to the irritation of my erstwhile junior college friends, I stopped using marijuana and other drugs—and that was the end of my connection with them. I began to volunteer at the Bookstore and said goodbye to my psychiatrist. Meher Baba was describing a path toward wellness, health, sanity, reality and truth and I was hopeful. Yet the desperation persisted inside me.

I was the on duty person Sundays at the Bookstore but typically over the hours of my watch it was unusual that anyone would venture in. One Sunday afternoon the desperation gnawing at me was particularly agonizing. I cried out to Meher Baba, Help me! Somehow! Someway! Help!

Within moments an older man walked in. We spoke briefly. I was my typically awkward self but he gave me his card and said,

"When you're ready, give me a call."

As desperate as I was, it still took a good six months to work up the courage. When I did finally approach him, he wasted no time in introducing me to the 12-step program of Alcoholics Anonymous. For the next three years, he was my spiritual guide. At AA meetings I identified with the spiritual sickness of recovering alcoholics but not with their physical symptoms, as I realized I was not an alcoholic myself, but was likewise suffering from a disease of the spirit—without the physical addiction part.

My mentor was kind and loving. He took me under his wing and gave freely of his time. He spoke of the spiritual path, describing a way of life that would relieve my miseries, make me happy and bring me closer to God. In light of Meher Baba's teachings, he revised AAs Step 2 from: "Came to believe that a Power Greater than ourselves could restore us to sanity" to "...restore us to RE-ALITY." I was 'in' with this mysterious idea of being restored to REALITY (whatever that is), on board with my mentor and committed to the 12-Step program; but I was not in all the way.

One evening after about six months, I was standing around talking to friends after an AA meeting. My mentor overheard me whining about my life and how things were not going well. He got in my face and said,

"Make up your mind what you want. If you want success in the world, there are many who can help you. If you want God, maybe I can be of some assistance, but don't waste my time!"

I couldn't have been more shocked. I had received an ultimatum! I desperately wanted what he had, but I clearly needed a push. The next day I drove out to the desert—past the endless suburbs and beyond the encircling mountains. Out where there was no trace of civilization, I stood alone on the desert floor and reached out to God with every last fiber of my being. I wasn't really aware of it at the time, but I had surrendered. With that, I got the grace to become teachable, the determination to go to any length for spiritual awakening and the sincerity to be fearless.

Over the next couple of years, God gave me the priceless gifts of an awakened heart and a clear head as He set my feet upon the path to Infinite Love.

*****

Raymond and his wife relocated to Asheville, North Carolina in 2016. Semi-retired, he now works part-time as a web designer/videographer and full-time as an explorer of the spiritual life.

101 Tales of Finding Love

MY JOURNEY HOME:
A Tale of Dust and Grit

by Evie Lindemann

Meher Baba 1929

Evie Lindemann 2016

The United States. Europe. Israel. Cyprus. Turkey. Iran. Afghanistan. Pakistan. India. Nepal. India. Nearly every border crossing looks alike. Dusty. Barbed wire. Soldiers. Documents. Strange languages. It was my habit, at each border, to bury a seed or a stone in the soil of the next country and say a silent prayer. "If there is anything true in the universe, any force that is genuine and true, any presence with ultimate meaning, I ask that you reveal yourself to me."

And now, backwards in time. It was two a.m. in the middle of the week, in a boarding house in Berkeley on the south side of the University of California, where I was an undergraduate student. I stayed up late each night, smoking in a darkened parlor, asking myself questions that seemed to have no answers. "Who am I?" "Why am I even here?" "Does anything matter?" The door opened and someone entered the space. She sat in another corner of the room and lit a cigarette. I watched as the tip burned glowing red and the smoke curled upward. She noticed the ember of mine and we began a conversation that continued into the wee hours of the next morning. We shared a few secrets. Deanna told me about a group that met in San Francisco regularly. She mentioned names. Murshida Duce. Meher Baba. Allan Cohen. Later on, she entrusted me with a box of items that contained a small book on Meher Baba, some photos, and some letters. She told me she couldn't keep them, and she asked if I would. I said yes. I tucked the box into my dresser drawer and never opened it again. It felt too private. She also suggested I go talk to Allan Cohen, who was easy to talk to, she said, and had an office on campus at the University of California Counseling Center. She described him to me.

I stood outside the building one late afternoon in the fall of 1967, waiting for him to emerge from his office at the end of the day. Too embarrassed to enter the Center, I hid behind a large barrier of bushes through which I could see. One by one, these mental health professionals exited the building. Finally, a man who more or less fit Deanna's description began walking down the pathway. As he neared my hiding place, I leapt onto the path in front of him. I asked, with some urgency in my voice, "Are you Allan Cohen?"

With a startled look on his face, and then a quick recovery, he replied: "Why, yes."

"I need to talk to you."

"It looks like you need to talk to me right now."

"I do."

"I'll tell you what. I have a few errands to run. You can come with me, and afterwards we can go to the International House of Pancakes and we'll talk about your concerns." Over dinner, he invited me to make a formal appointment with him at the Center.

In my first session with Allan, I noticed a huge photograph of a smiling man behind his chair. The look of immense joy on the man's face irritated me. How could this unknown man be that happy when I felt so miserable? Sometime later, I asked Allan: "Who is that guy?" He shared a few things about this man, whose name was Meher Baba. Later, I remembered reading in the *Daily Californian* that Meher Baba had died. I continued my sessions with Allan, who helped me find some order in my chaotic life. During that time my father, still in his early fifties, took his own life. This was a devastating blow for me, one which I carried with me to all those dusty roadside border crossings.

After graduation, I traveled around Europe and North Africa, finally ending up on a kibbutz in Israel. During those warm days when I harvested eggplant, grapefruit and bananas, an idea slowly arose in my mind. I should go to India and find Meher Baba's place. In some letters between Allan and me during my travels, he answered a few more questions I had about Meher Baba. Even if he had died, I reasoned that I still needed to go there. I convinced a friend, Richard, that he should go too.

My kibbutz had bomb shelters that we sometimes had to run to when the kibbutz was shelled. Located south of the Sea of Galilee, near the Jordanian border, it was in a prime location for target practice by enemies of Israel. During a shelling the buildings shook. Occasionally I would get word in the dining hall that a kibbutznik had stepped on a land mine and his life was ended. The dangers of the place didn't register, really. I was too young and still felt immortal, and I was unable to appreciate that I could be in the dead man's shoes just as easily. After my six-month commitment ended, I left the kibbutz with a new pair of sandals, their parting gift to me. Richard and I sailed to Cyprus in April 1970 to get new passports with no markings of Israeli stamps, as our plan was to travel overland through the Middle East.

Along the way, we experimented with many kinds of drugs that were readily available. Marijuana. Opium. LSD (popularly known as acid). Books were passed from hand to hand along that trail of young hippies, all of us searching for something or hiding from ourselves. I remember reading *Siddhartha, Autobiography of a Yogi*, and *Steppenwolf*.

In Pakistan, the day before we entered India, I received a timely letter from Allan with instructions on how to get to Ahmednagar, along with contact information for Adi K. Irani, Meher Baba's personal secretary. We went to Goa first, a hippy haven along the west central coast of India. We rented a shack on the beach for a few rupees per month and helped the fishermen pull in their catch for our evening meal. We continued our experiments with acid in our quest for meaning and found that our 'trips' were becoming less alluring, more negative. One day a French friend told us that a woman connected with Meher Baba had arrived on the beach. She introduced us to Virginia Small, who was recovering from a broken leg.

In all our travels through India, we had never encountered a single book by Meher Baba. Virginia had one with her entitled *The Advancing Stream of Life*, which she lent us. We devoured the book in a single afternoon, looked at each other, and declared: "Let's leave tomorrow." On the steamer that took us to Bombay, as it was called then, we decided to walk to the far end of the ship and dump our drugs overboard into the Arabian Sea. We were not aware at that time of Baba's warnings about drugs. And we also decided, just in case this Meher Baba turned out to be bogus, to save two tabs of acid.

When we arrived in Ahmednagar at the end of 1970, there were few Westerners there—perhaps a handful at most. We thought we needed a living Master, and since Meher Baba was no longer living we planned to stay only a few days and then continue our search. With each meeting of a different close member of Meher Baba's circle, something began to happen to me. Each one, so unique yet so special, made me realize I'd like to stay around to soak up whatever this something special was that they each possessed. An image arose in my mind of a beautiful piece of jewelry set with different gemstones, each one a unique cut of brilliant color. Amartithi came and went and we made nearly daily visits to Meherazad by bicycle. With practically unlimited access to the mandali, to their stories, and to the sparkling quality of love they embodied, I began to fall in love with Meher Baba. We flushed our two remaining tabs of acid down an Indian-style toilet in a local hotel one hot afternoon. I was finally home. Those prayers at each border crossing had been heard by Him, and that changed everything.

*****

Evie Lindemann now lives in New Haven, Connecticut, where she is an Associate Professor in a graduate program of art therapy at Albertus Magnus College. Printmaking enlivens her spirit and helps her to find balance between the mind and the heart. She has worked with combat veterans, hospice patients, students, and many other groups, all of whom have helped her to express the creative impulse inherent in being human.

101 Tales
of Finding Love

INSIDE OUT,
UPSIDE DOWN

by Claire Mataira

Meher Baba circa 1966

Meher Baba
Australia   feb-march
                1996

Meher Baba newsletter

Artwork © Claire Mataira

I t was October 13, 1974 in Adelaide, Australia, when my first husband and I had been invited to visit some friends from the College of the Arts, where we were both students, for a birthday party. We sat around the large kitchen table with about fourteen people and had something to eat and drink. Then the host brought out a bottle of a special brew and he gave some to each person and we had a toast to the Birthday Boy. After that we all got a little tipsy and we went to sit in different places, some chatting in small groups.

I looked around the house and wandered into a smallish room that had been constructed within the large hallway with grocery boxes—this room had been painted completely white on the inside. To add to the impression of starkness there was no furniture in this room except for a white fridge and a single mattress on the floor. The bed was covered with a white sheet, and at the far end of the room a very large poster of a black and white photographic portrait adorned the wall. I sat down on the floor to enjoy the uplifting energy of that makeshift room, and as I did so, the face on the photograph seemed to speak to me, in a wordless way, by giving me a vision.

I saw in my mind's eye a band of pure living energy that coursed through all of time and space, and to me this seemed like the Tree of Life. The branches on that tree were the many divine incarnations on our earth during this procession of time, as the Word of God was born in human form many times, to interact with His creation. As each human incarnation of God died, He left the imprint of His face on this Tree of Life. The memory of all these faces was then stored in our collective human unconscious memory. We knew this divine Being as "The Ancient One," the One Who comes again and again, and I was looking at a picture of one of these faces!

I was quite amazed at that, and I said to Him; "I know You so well!" and He seemed to reply, "And I know YOU so well!"

I got lost in this encounter and spent the whole time of my visit there by myself in that white room, contemplating this face, as it continued to give me other insights about the evolution of consciousness! Then somebody came to tell me that it was time to leave. I went close to the poster to see whether there was more information on it. There were only two words printed at the bottom of that photograph.

These words were, "MEHER BABA."

The next day I went to the only place that I thought might help me, The American Bookshop in Adelaide. I went in and asked; "Do you have any books on Meher Baba?"

"Sure," was the answer. "Over there."

I had a cursory look at the material, but one book had already taken my attention; it was the book called *Avatar* by Jean Adriel. "This is it," I thought, and I bought it. I spent the next few days reading it, and while doing so I started to make a painting using the portrait photo in the front of the book.

I alternated painting with reading and I was very taken by it all. Jean Adriel had had many unusual spiritual experiences in her life and her descriptions of these bore a resemblance to some of the things my husband and I had experienced. As I read this book I found out that Meher Baba had transcended his body in 1969. It was now 1974. Somehow I had been looking for the face of the Christ ever since I was very young and now He had come and gone, without inviting me to meet Him! I felt He had not cared about my heartfelt wish, and I experienced deep disappointment and wept bitterly.

The next night I had a very curious dream. I dreamt that I was standing in a dark place but a bright light was shining on me. I felt very self-conscious. Then I saw Meher Baba walk towards me. He was about thirty years old and his long hair was loose around his shoulders. His clothes were shining white. He had with Him a group of disciples, who were carrying palm fronds like I imagined they would have done when Jesus entered Jerusalem. They were all dressed in white. Meher Baba turned to his disciples and made a gesture for them to stay behind.

Then He walked towards me with a powerful gait. He came right up to me and stood before me. I was feeling stunned, petrified and amazed all at the same time. He took both my hands in His. He looked me in the eyes and said, *I will turn your life inside out and upside down.* With that He tugged me by the hands and threw me up in the air. I somersaulted but still He held on to my hands. He somersaulted after me, but I was the first to land hard on my back, absolutely winded. To top it all, Baba then came hurtling after me and landed headlong into my heart!!

I woke with a shock. "I am going to die," was my first thought. I fought for my breath and my heart felt crushed and numb. Never before had I had a dream with so much impact! I was shocked to the depths of my being. But I slowly recovered in the following hours.

In the months that were to come, He got busy with his promise—to totally upset my life. So when things became extremely difficult in my life, and I started to lose all the things I had strived for, and lost the friends I had counted on, I knew who was to blame for this: Meher Baba!!

The first time He 'spoke' to me, I was looking at a large poster; this poster was printed in rather harsh black and white tones, but still, it had captured me. I found out that these posters were for sale at a local 'alternative' gift shop, and I bought one, to work out what exactly it was that had fascinated me so.

This picture turned out to be my 'battleground' with Baba: it seemed that Baba could look 'daggers and storm clouds' at me. It appeared as if He mirrored any negativity that I harbored inside me! I had no one that I could talk to about this process and I had no previous experience of anything like this, so I just wrestled with this picture in my heart and mind.

That year, 1974, I had done many esoteric oil paintings and presented them at the last assessment in the final year of my Art studies. I thought it looked rather impressive, all those wonderful shapes and colours; it was a robust body of work. When it was time to discuss my display in front of the panel of teachers and experts, I went ahead and explained all the thoughts and intuitions that were behind the paintings, which really was my spiritual search.

Their faces grew troubled. Then came the verdict, "It would have been better if you hadn't tried to explain it; there is no clear theme throughout the work and you haven't built up any personal style. Moreover, you have been absent from school rather a lot while working at home. You have FAILED."

I was very disappointed and could not understand how this could be. But there it was, and the appropriate papers arrived duly by mail a week or so later.

In the first painting that I made of Meher Baba, I put myself and husband, our animals and friends and family in His arms. For that I gave Baba several arms and hands! I also envisaged that Baba wears 'Illusion' like a cloak, with the stars on the hem of His garment. At the very top of the painting I wrote, "When, oh my everlasting sweet Lord?" It indicated how sad I was that I had missed out meeting Him in this incarnation and that now I may have to wait many lifetimes again.

But in my 'inside out upside down' dream Baba had made it very clear to me that He did not need to be incarnated to have a very strong presence in my life. Later I came to understand that 'to remember Him' makes Him present, because He is primarily a spiritual being, and will be with us, whenever we ask Him to be a part of our lives.

One of the friends we had made while studying had started to grow some marihuana plants on the bushy edge of our rented, forested hillside property; the property owners sent the police around and we were taken to court for 'growing dope.'

While in court we saw this friend in the foyer and said, "Don't you want to own up to growing this, because you did this and you are in for it already anyway?" He said he was into it up to his ears and could not take this on as well. We were loyal and never mentioned his name, but we said a friend grew the plants. Strangely enough, later in the procedure, the policeman bringing the evidence told the court that he had left it on the roof of his car for a moment and it had been blown away by a gust of wind! Everyone in court had difficulty keeping a straight face! I suspected the unseen world of spirit having a hand in it. In the end, after seven months (!!) of being in court, we were given a small fine and the judge threw out the case; all they had was our honest story, but no evidence!

The landlord of our hillside cottage wanted us out of the property, really because they wanted to upgrade it and sell it, but he said it was because we had been growing drugs. Again I was disappointed because we had signed a legal paper that we could stay there for five years. Our lawyer said we could fight it in court, but I was tired of court cases and opted to abandon that idea.

So we moved out and went to share a house with husband's brother in Adelaide. I was very sad to leave the cottage and the life we had there, and the animals had to be given away. Husband decided that now was the time for spiritual practice and became celibate! He went to sleep somewhere else on a permanent basis and I felt really abandoned. All this was Baba's first sweep at 'turning my life upside down!!'

As exciting as the previous year of painting and discovery had been, so was this year dismal and hopeless. We seemed to have lost our drive and neither of us wanted to try and redo our failed final exam subjects. The Court cases about the marihuana growing had left us feeling bad and depleted. Our marriage felt like a lie. Our country cottage dream of living on the land with our trees and animals had evaporated.

While all this was going on I was reading the Baba books over and over. I started on the *Discourses* and tried very hard to assimilate what was being conveyed. I was coming into a new world, a new way of living. Nothing was like it used to be. All my beliefs and ideas from the past did not seem to fit anymore. Things I had taken for granted suddenly looked different in a new light of understanding. And that understanding did not come instantly, either. Sometimes I felt I was just groping in the dark for new points of reference, which were not what I had been taught up to that date. To enlarge my basis of understanding I also started going to the Theosophical Society in Adelaide and borrowed books from their library. I read books about saints and masters of all sorts of different religions. We still continued to hope, looking for some group or place to relate to, to find some people who had similar experiences or also felt drawn to Meher Baba.

After I had read my first book about Meher Baba, I found a Californian address in the back of the book, and had written to them. They had replied by telling me that there were some followers of Meher Baba in Sydney, connected with a place called Meher House in Beacon Hill. I wrote to them also, feeling that Sydney was as far away as anything could be—more than a thousand kilometers!

I had forgotten about that letter, in my gloomy state, and it was just one of those nights. My husband and one of our friends had gone to satsang, a gathering of followers of Maharaj Ji, to see what that would be like. I had stayed home with husband's brother, who was playing on his electric guitar with headphones on. Suddenly there was a knock on the door! I thought, "Maybe they have come back home early," but it was somebody else. Two people rather, and I had never seen them before in my life. I stared at them nonplussed.

"Are you the person who wrote to Meher House in Sydney?" one of them asked me.

"Yes," I said.

"My name is Peter Rowan and I work for Meher Handcrafts in Sydney. I came here to do some business and was told to look you up. With me is Anthony Mellowship who lives in Adelaide with his wife. I have some information for you and a short movie of Meher Baba!"

Of course we were happily surprised and invited the men in for tea and bikkies. Anthony went and got the movie projector from the car. It was a heavy thing and the roll of film contained three minutes of movie. We had watched it several times when my husband and our friend came home from satsang. Of course they had to watch it too, and it was some time before we let our guests go! It gave me some consolation that Meher Baba was also reaching out to us in the form of other people, and on another occasion Peter brought Steve Hein, again on a business visit, to meet with us and share some Baba stories.

This was our first contact with other followers of Meher Baba. And it was also the first movie I saw of Meher Baba; He was walking like I had seen in my dream—with a white garment and flowing long hair, striding strong and gracefully in the middle of a group of disciples!

*****

Claire Mataira is now living in the upper Amazon region of Peru, near Iquitos. She works with medicinal plants of that region. She has some interviews on YouTube.

101 Tales of Finding Love

HOW I MET THE MASTER

by Lou McKenzie

"Meher Baba"
1932
(New York)

Claire
8 april 2005

Artwork © Claire Mataira

Lou McKenzie

My journey to the Avatar Meher Baba began as a child with the biblical teachings of Jesus. It's important to know that I was born in 1948, in Oak Ridge, Tennessee, just after the atomic bomb was made by man. My mother and father's seeds were poisoned and I was born with the same heavy metals and chemicals inside of me that created the atomic bomb. My organs were affected and I grew up with many health challenges—until the day came that I had to start pulling them out. Being born with these toxins and pulling them out is part of my story about meeting Meher Baba.

All those toxins created major trauma in my body and brain—Post Traumatic Stress Disorder. Fast forward to the early nineties, when I paid my first visit to the Meher Spiritual Center in Myrtle Beach. I didn't have a clue about Baba then, only that the Center would provided solitude and the ocean—a place to heal. It was His plan for me at birth.

For years my life was in chaos, and my mother was going insane. I was her caretaker, but by this time, I was also feeling that I was losing my mind. Many, many times I felt the urge to commit suicide but my love for Baba and His teachings kept me from doing it. I have always felt that I was in God's hands, but it wasn't until after Mother died in 2013 that I asked Baba to come into my heart. Once Mother passed and with Him in my heart, I brought Him home. I began in earnest to study *God Speaks* and many other books written about Avatar Meher Baba.

Meher Baba has been with me since birth. And in 2010, when I began pulling the heavy metals out of me, I now know that Baba was in charge of my healing in total. It's been very slow and I have experienced much suffering due to my drainer organs having been effected by the toxins at birth—especially my heart and brain. My understanding of it all now is this: as those toxins were removed, so were many sanskaras. And in the place of those toxins, Baba has filled me with His grace and intuition. What has occurred is

191

ongoing and these things I'm sharing are what I know in this present time. As I study and read more and learn more and more about Avatar Meher Baba, my understanding will change.

Each of us has a very personal relationship with God. I don't believe we are supposed to talk about it except when the opportunity is right for sharing. So, that is why I am sharing here and in the Facebook group—How I Met the Master—tell your story and it will help us all because it is a safe place and those that ask are trustworthy and it may help others.

Thank you so much for allowing me this opportunity to share. Jai Baba

*****

Presently I live in Sale Creek, Tennessee, just north of Chattanooga. If it is Baba's Divine Wish, my husband and I will move to Asheville, North Carolina in the future.

101 Tales of Finding Love

HIDE AND SEEK

by Jim Migdoll

Jim Migdoll late 1960s

Jim Migdoll

Jim Migdoll at home in Australia

When I first met Eruch and he asked me how I came to Baba, I basically told him it was a long, drawn out game of Hide and Seek. How very many hints and signs Baba gave me, and yet how long it took to finally come to Him. Eruch replied, "Why didn't you just run to Him?" My mind went blank for a few seconds and my reply seemed to just spring spontaneously from within, "Well, I suppose I did—but in His time." Eruch beamed! Re-enforcing my theory that he had an uncanny knack of asking the perfect question, which would allow us to come up with the perfect answer! I think all of the Mandali did this.

In 1961 or '62, an adolescent male in Kettering, Ohio was home alone, in the middle of the day, watching TV—something he never did. A man in a classroom setting was talking about the life and work of the Silent Messiah, Meher Baba. The young man was rocked to his foundations. Inexplicably very angry, confused, and torn up inside. He didn't remember the incident again until some years later.

After dropping out of my second year at Memphis State University, I hit the hippie trail with great expectations! Woodstock, the Chicago riots, Haight-Ashbury, Greenwich Village and so on. I swallowed the psychedelic utopianism chimera—hook, line and sinker. Really believed in lasting enlightenment through drugs! In 1967 while hitchhiking in California I saw His Face for the second time. The *Don't Worry be Happy* card. I just had to have it. The driver of the car was reluctant to part with it and I had to almost beg him for it. From that moment on He was with me. During many lost drug moments I would pull the card out with a flourish and show it around. It was one of my prized possessions throughout the hippie years.

In 1968 a longing to go to India reached a point of obsession. The desire was so strong that I determined to even cut my hair and get a job! I only stuck it out long enough to raise money for Mexico. Thus began the greatest adventure of my hippie career. Living on a vast, wild and unspoiled beach of great beauty, we surfed and smoked. My best friend shared my obsession to get to India and we would lie awake under the stars making pacts to get there no matter what it took. This soul-deep desperate longing took place precisely during the Last Darshan! We did return to America and got jobs, but then spent the money on drugs.

It's easy to say, "Well, the time wasn't right," but I actually feel that if I could have mustered up the strength and courage necessary to get to India by *hook or crook*, He would have drawn me straight to Guruprasad.

In early 1970 it was time to flee the polluted city. Set up a commune. Grow organic food. In the desert outside Phoenix, Arizona were some abandoned gold mines called the Robot Mines. (The eccentric owner designed robots to fight wars so men wouldn't have to!) As with so many 'communes,' the drug lethargy meant that only one person really worked. The total darkness within those caves was a metaphor for our collective consciousness. Dull, confused and stoned.

One day light appeared! A large man in a VW van came to spend a night or two. He kept repeating that he was "going to Alaska to find God," and he would proudly show how he'd outfitted his van for the journey. Initially I was completely repulsed by this guy. He was big and loud and laughed very hard. Stomped around the place laughing. It was quite disruptive to our 'cool', our spiritual torpor and drug haze.

BUT, slowly my repulsion changed to awe. Here was a child in the biblical sense. Spontaneous, happy and radiant. One day I saw him reading and decided that whatever it was I'd find it and read it. The first chance I had I snuck up to his backpack and rummaged through for the aqua-colored book. The *Discourses* by Meher Baba. Subsequently I found someone who had the *Discourses* and I borrowed them. But just as with the *Don't Worry be Happy* card (where I would attempt to read the quote on the back, "To penetrate into the essence...") the material simply wouldn't penetrate! It's impossible to explain but I just couldn't comprehend what I was reading. It was as if Baba had erected an invisible barrier to intellectual understanding.

When Yogi Bhajan came to America from India, with a mission to get young people off drugs, he sent one of his first students (BabaDon) to Phoenix, Arizona to teach *'Kundalini'* yoga in 1970. It was the beginning of the end of my search for God through drugs. I was detoxed by hours and hours of intense yoga and breathing exercises, vegetarian diet, fasting, etc. We held yoga classes at the Arizona State University and every time I'd go there I would first stop at the library, get the copy of *God Speaks* and open it to the photo of Baba on the tiger skin. I would stare and stare with an almost blank mind. A deep, deep wordless questioning—kind of like, "Who are you," and "Why am I drawn to sit here and stare at your photo?!" Then I'd turn a few pages, attempt to read some, shake my head in confusion and go back to staring at the photo.

After about six months my yoga teacher ordered me to go teach on my own. I picked Memphis where I had lived through high school, college and the early hippie years. Thus I began a short career as a mini-yogi guru! Actually in retrospect I can see Baba's Hand in those free yoga classes in the park. Overweight housewives, lawyers, hippies, children and athletes—we were all one. Chanting to God. Sufi dancing. Hugging, and doing yoga. *The most beautiful group experiences I've ever had.* Almost all of the students immediately took to heart my message to give up drugs, and they did.

One of the students was a very eccentric, leprechaun-like fellow. Bradley approached me one day before class in a virtual frenzy. He was so excited as he ran up to me and started tugging on my yoga whites, repeating over and over, "Jim, Meher Baba's God! Meher Baba's God! Look, I've got all the information here. I wrote off to California. Look. Jim, Meher Baba's God!"

This cool unaffected 'yogi guru' finally calmed Bradley down with the promise that he'd read the literature, an info packet from PO

Box 1101 in Berkeley. Again, it simply wouldn't penetrate. I tried to read it, but would just drift off. [By this time the reader may be thinking, "My God, what's it gonna take for this guy to open his eyes and ears!"]

Baba gave me hints, clues, and signs in abundance and I still stumbled on obliviously. There are only two possible conclusions: 1) How could anybody be so damn thick? So blind? 2) Meher Baba's timing is precise and Perfect—so much so that He can temporarily suspend the entire workings of a reasonably healthy mind and intellect—until He deems it the right time. I hope it's the second alternative.

At some point I decided that Memphis had to have a vegetarian restaurant and we, the yoga class, would open it. One of my students who came religiously with her two young daughters, was married to a multi-millionaire—he bought us a restaurant! We transformed a Southern-style rib shack into a vegetarian restaurant. (Purified the oven that used to roast the pork by sitting inside it and chanting!) For the first month or two of business, Patanjali's Pure Food Restaurant had the purest energy and most exalted 'vibes' of any place of business I've ever been in. It really was a temple. I'm sure it was due to our 'unknown Guest.'

Before opening I wrote to Meher Baba Information in Berkeley and bought five hundred *Don't Worry be Happy* cards, and every single poster that they had. I think we also bought *God Speaks* and the *Discourses*. I decorated the restaurant and besides the hundreds of photos of the yoga class I put up all of the Baba posters. One wall in particular became a saint/master/guru collage. From Yogananda to Jesus and Mary. Sri Ramakrishna, Yogi Bhajan, and any and all pictures of spiritual figures I could get—all went up on this wall. I arranged it personally. Guess Who ended up on top? *The Don't Worry* be Happy poster and the *Not We But One* poster! I used to gaze up and silently ask, "Who are you and why are you on top?"

I directed Mark, the cashier, to be sure that every single person got a *Don't Worry be Happy* card when they paid. Mark had gradually slipped into an exalted spiritual state that he wouldn't discuss. He would just radiate love and light! Quite extraordinary. I used to secretly watch him from a distance and feel uplifted. Now what do you think he was reading? The *Discourses* of course! I asked him about them and Meher Baba, but he was so tight-lipped about his inner life that I couldn't get much out of him.

One day I got a phone call. The operator said, "I have a collect call from Meher Baba, will you accept the charges?" It was a Baba lover in Oklahoma who had heard about this restaurant filled with Baba's photos. (I later found out it was Max Reif.) Imagine his chagrin when I insisted it was a yoga ashram restaurant. It reached the absurd point where I asked Malcolm, the cook to read *God Speaks* for me! ... and tell me who or what '*Avatar*' was.

Eventually the tiny seeds of hypocrisy in me grew enormous. Having set myself up as a spiritual figure, I had to pay the price. I won't go into the gory details, but I experienced first hand the terrible dangers of trying to be a 'guru' or spiritual teacher. In desperation I decided to go back and get 're-inspired' by my teacher who was a very strong and disciplined man. When I got to Phoenix it turned out to be auspicious timing. A huge yoga gathering was being held in the Arizona desert at a place called Crown King. Students of this 3HO Yoga group came from all over the country. We chanted, yoga'd and got high naturally.

Three days later coming down the mountain, we stopped at a country store for lunch—the only store for miles around. The proprietor was not an ordinary country store proprietor. She was a large, radiant woman whose skin shone. She exuded a powerful spiritual presence. In fact she was probably the most beautiful and powerful person I'd ever met. We all immediately began to talk about God and spirituality and she recounted the numerous ashrams she had lived in, and the gurus she had met and studied with during the forties and fifties.

Jim Migdoll

I don't remember how it came up, but since I had been asking people for years what they knew about Meher Baba, I must have said something to her. At one point she looked at me and said, "And that's when I met your friend—in San Francisco."

My heart was hammering. I was dizzy with anticipation. I felt my search was at an end. At last here was someone who had actually met Baba. She would tell me all about Him. I struggled to regain my yoga cool, and tried desperately to ask in a casual fashion, "Uhhh, could you tell us about the time you met Meher Baba?"

She looked deep into my eyes and a smile grew bigger and bigger across her face as she slowly shook her head from side to side. Wouldn't say a word! We went on to other things.

My God, the lengths He will go to, to insure His perfect timing.

When I returned to Memphis, the restaurant had gone downhill. People were smoking pot again. My friend/students gradually turned against me. It all fell apart and I left town in shame. This tiny payback for being a hypocritical 'teacher' was so small compared to what it could have been. It was Baba's Grace for sure.

I fled to San Francisco and put the *Don't Worry be Happy* poster from the restaurant up on my wall. I would stare and stare at it, knowing and feeling intuitively that His eyes were tunnels to Infinity. I kept procrastinating going to Berkeley to get a book and finally get to the bottom of this. Eventually I did go and bought *Listen, Humanity*. Every word sank deep into my soul. My heart opened. He came in. We started our honeymoon together. My life began.

*****

My wife Tricia and I now live on the Sunshine Coast (Woombye) very near Avatars Abode. We recently finished what I call Phase I in working with the Archive collection at the Abode of written material by and about Baba. Like everybody else ... trying hard to hold tight to our Beloved's *daaman*!

101 Tales of Finding Love

IN SLOW MOTION

by Karl Moeller

Don Stevens, Karl Moeller, and Irma Sheppard,
on the Beads On One String pilgrimage,
Mt. Abu, Rajasthan, 2010

Karl Moeller

THE MUSLIM ADHAN, CALL TO PRAYER

Come to prayer. Come to prayer.
Come to Success. Come to Success.
Allah is Most Great. Allah is Most Great.
There is none worthy of being worshipped except Allah.

My first awareness of Meher Baba was in early 1968, in a suburb north of Detroit, Michigan. I was sporadically attending college, working in a print shop, taking whatever soft drugs I could find, drawing obsessively, working on cars, and playing keyboards in a band. A year before, that band had played the Grande Ballroom, Detroit's answer to San Francisco's Fillmore and Avalon ballrooms. I have the poster, a part of Detroit music history. A full life for an eighteen-year-old 'weekend hippie.'

Because of undiagnosed Attention Deficit Disorder, school had been a prison sentence for me. I was also the first teen I knew whose parents had divorced. It was so unusual in those days that in retrospect it was akin to being illegitimate. So things in the parental household were and had been pretty glum for a long time, despite being middle class and financially comfortable. It seems now that I had been mildly depressed for years.

Being a musician in the sixties, I obviously had peers with access to various mind-altering substances. We indulged in psychedelics in quiet, composed circumstances as well as in the euphoric energy of the many Midwest music festivals. I have seen virtually every sixties rock act worth mentioning. I joined that tribal life quite enthusiastically; it was a huge and fun contrast to the mind-numbing conformity of the Detroit suburbs. As an artist and musician, there was the persistent illusion of drug-enhanced creativity, which gave these euphoric states an extra level of appeal. I never came close to having a bad trip. I never saw universes, or the face of God. It was more a gentle softening of reality's edges. Gently flowing rug patterns, a geometric order to clouds in the sky. A newness of experience. I came to prize the quiet ecstasy of psychedelics, and missed it when I 'came down.' Often, while tripping, I simply couldn't stop smiling.

Because of the Beatles' influence, along with most of the hip generation, I was quite aware of India; *yogis* and others from India were promising mental and spiritual breakthroughs, without the use of drugs. I wanted those *siddhis*! Having been a child in the fifties, reading comic books, I was predisposed to believe in superpowers, in the ultimate self-improvement project. There was quite a bit of drug-fueled grandiosity going on, naïvely assuming that yogic powers were attainable to Westerners at all. This manifested in listening to ragas on the stereo (as if that would do it) and reading everything I could.

I recall reading Lobsang Rampa's *Easy Journey to Other Planets*, and various Krishna Consciousness books, which promised *satchitananda*, Eternal Conscious Bliss. Sign me up! Of course we all read Yogananda's wonderful autobiography, with its own miracles and time-traveling super-yogi Babaji. The Yogananda Self Realization Fellowship group had very well-attended Sunday lectures near downtown at the Detroit Art Institute, and some of us went down once a month to hear Oliver Black, an early, senior disciple of Yogananda's, speak.

Through a mutual friend, sometime in the winter of 1967-68, I met two brothers, Michael and David. After getting to know one another and going to the Grande Ballroom and various Midwest rock festivals, they invited me to move in and share rent in a dark green house in a dark green area of a northern suburb, Birmingham, Michigan, on dark green tree-lined Lincoln Avenue. I had one of the upstairs bedrooms. We called it the 'Lincoln house.'

Michael was exactly one year older (we share a birthday), David one year younger, a drummer. Michael's partner, Trisha, a ballet and dance instructor, was the 'house mother,' keeping all these loons grounded, cooking near-infinite variations on brown rice dishes. The household was probably typical of the counterculture in those days, older rented home, some old furniture, oriental rugs, garish India prints, concert flyers and black-light posters on the walls, incense, and as I said, lots of brown rice. Ragas and blues on the record player. I tend to prize friendships, and David and I remain in regular touch. He recently helped me reconstruct some of the dynamics of that household, specifically the source of the small trove of books on by or about Meher Baba. Trisha's Aunt Lea, whom I don't recall but must've met, was their Baba contact there in Michigan, and was the source of the books on Baba.

What Baba books were available in 1968? Certainly Jean Adriel's *Avatar.* I can't imagine having tried to brave *God Speaks.* Probably Charles Purdom's *The God-Man.* Certainly the *Discourses.* I recall reading about Baba's teasing statements that he would break his silence, most notably at the Hollywood Bowl, which, among other similar events, never took place.

I will say this was a rather reflective bunch of hippies, not prone to loud partying, except very occasionally. Quite bright and interesting minds. Either Trisha or Michael might have been inclined to discuss these ideas, but I have no memory of discussing this particular branch of spirituality with anyone while living in that house. Either Baba's instructions regarding drugs didn't appear in my reading, or I glossed right over them, because we smoked whatever grass or hash came around, plus some notable forays into psychedelics. At this stage of the narrative I may as well admit it, yes, drugs, psychedelics, opened my way—eventually—to Meher Baba. He'll use *anything.* What was initially spiritual greed for siddhis gradually mutated into something quite different.

While nostalgia gives a rosy glow to those long-gone days—the camaraderie, the flowering of a generation, the glorious outpouring of music everywhere—there was another, uglier side of the sixties. There were race riots in Detroit and elsewhere, assassinations, poverty in the inner cities, the constant threat of drug busts, and hostile police were in our faces every day. Outside of home, a longhair had to be alert. For my cohort, males between eighteen and twenty-five, there was also the ever-present threat of Selective Service. The draft board would summon us to the dread 'pre-induction physical.' Based on that physical, they had the legal right to shove us into one of the branches of the armed forces, or send us to jail. The hippie generation was uniquely attuned to and disgusted by America's clear aggression and empire-building. Vietnam.

'The War,' as we called it, was one of the most radicalizing events for my generation, along with the positive ones: the Beatles, the emergence of rock music, ready access to drugs, and a free, seductive, colorful lifestyle, especially compared to the button-down conformity of our parents' generation. It was obvious to me that I wanted nothing to do with the military, regardless of the unjustifiable war in Vietnam. So while it appeared that I assiduously sought, and obtained, a permanent deferment, in retrospect I see it was Meher Baba's grace. I was then free of the threat of the draft, some time before the draft 'lottery' system was instituted.

At such a distance in time, chronology gets hazy. 1968 passed. Sometime in February 1969, Michael told me that he'd heard via Aunt Lea that Meher Baba had passed away. Without breaking his silence, obviously. I had to digest this for a while. I had really resonated with what I'd read about Baba, especially the hopeful message about the changes in humanity to be brought about by his breaking silence. By this time, the stories about the Beatles' estrangement from the Maharishi were well known. The Maharishi Mashesh Yogi was presumed to have been sexual with one or more of the many young Western women in his ashram in India. John Lennon had been quite vocal about his opinion, and we knew that the song "Sexy Sadie" off the Beatles' "White Album" was actually a thinly veiled attack on the Maharishi.

So I was well-primed for disappointment when I heard that Meher Baba had passed without breaking his silence—and without lifting humanity. I was quite bitter. I thought, "Just another Indian charlatan preying on Westerners' gullibility." Not me, not anymore.

*****

Living a hippie life there in the Lincoln house and working in a print shop, slowly failing out of college, I was simply marking time, until a confluence of events got me on a track to eventually earn a solid living and become a functioning adult. It seems to me now that Meher Baba arranged for me to get a year's computer training, business programming. In those days there were no specific computing degrees, no Master of Information Science, no computer science. The only way to do it was either become a math major—not bloody likely—or at a business school. So I did my year in business school, quite surprised to find I was a gifted coder and systems analyst, and after graduating got a short-term job, early wide area networking, for the school. They later referred me to a company where I found my first full-time job in computers.

That led directly to my ten years with a Chishti *murshid*.

The man I will refer to as Abdul Samad (slave of the Eternal) and I worked for the same Dearborn, Michigan automotive supplier starting in 1972. I was twenty-two. About the time I met Samad, I had discovered a new set of books, G.I. Gurdjieff and his acolytes Ouspensky and Orage. It became clear over time that Gurdjieff's teaching methods owed much to various Sufi Orders, mostly the Naqshbandi.

Samad was a Muslim Pakistani engineer in the United States, going to university as a grad student and working full time. Comparatively, Americans don't know how to work hard. He'd brought his wife and young son along. He read the Gurdjieff along with me, heavy going indeed, and we had many happy lunches in the shadow of the Ford Rouge auto plant, discussing various forms of spirituality and eating his wife's spicy goat-meat *samosas*.

Over time we moved on to Idries Shah's books, a wonderful introduction to the history and development of Islamic Sufism. Shah, in his enthusiasm for things Sufi, ascribed the preservation of science and literature in medieval Europe to hidden Sufi influence, and wrote at length about the near-magical capabilities of the evolved Sufi practitioner.

Yes, exactly like the siddhis of a few years earlier, I wanted that! I wanted *firasat*, intuitive insight. I wanted understanding of the *ahwal*, inner states. I wanted to benefit from and dispense *baraka*, power or blessing. Extremely naïve, yes, I was. But one starts from where one is. I still believed that spirituality was essentially the ultimate self-improvement. At that time I didn't understand that the spiritual life is one of loss.

We both became interested in Chishti Hazrat Inayat Khan's and Samuel L. (Sufi Ahmad Murad) Lewis's books. Lewis's various initiations by Indian and Pakistani Chishtis, Qadiris and Naqshbandis in his various visits to India in the early 1960s fired our imaginations. Finding an American who had been initiated this deeply into the heart of Sufism was very exciting. At that time, despite my reading about Inayat Khan and Sam Lewis, I was completely unaware of Murshida Rabia Martin, her connection with Inayat Khan's organization in the West, and of her later connection with Meher Baba. All that was years in the future.

A slight digression: what about drug use, especially psychedelics? Since I hadn't actually hung with Baba lovers nor continued my reading, I was unaware of Baba's dictum on drug use. The mental demands of programming and systems design for the early computers, all mainframes, soon made me realize that if I continued even sporadic use of psychedelics, I wouldn't be able to maintain the level of focus and energy required. Or show up for work regularly. A couple of other situations helped me to move away from tripping. I fancied myself a bit of an artist, and alternated between fairly disciplined realistic work and totally freeform expressionist or surrealist drawing. My surreal work sometimes became quite elaborate, filling entire sheets, taking dozens of hours. Once, while tripping, I spent some time working on a surreal drawing. Later, looking at it while straight, I was startled to realize that it looked very similar in approach and finish to my other surreal pieces, done *sans* psychedelics. Something akin to this happened when I made music recordings while high, and not high. It was clear that in music and art, at least, I didn't need to prop open the 'Doors Of Perception' with psychedelics. So I stopped. And kept my job. However, I did continue to smoke dope whenever it was available, and kept that up for another ten years or so.

After a couple of years of friendship, I discovered that Abdul Samad and his wife were longtime murids of a famous Chishti murshid in Karachi, Pakistan—Mohammed Jamil Arifi Sahib, 'Sarkar' to his followers. Sarkar had evidently been initiated into ten separate Sufi orders. I had some extraordinary dreams, and dreams are especially meaningful to Chishtis. Abdul Samad encouraged me to write them down and send them to Sarkar. The message came back: "clean your heart."

A small side trip—in my elementary school years my family lived in a two-story home about a quarter mile north of the Detroit Zoo. These were the years before central air conditioning, so on hot summer nights the windows were open. When the wind was right, it was like living on the African veldt. Lying in bed, I listened to coughing leopards, the cry of peacocks, elephants trumpeting and lions roaring. Perhaps as a result, I had many dreams where I was walking along the road just to the north of the Zoo, walking with my hand on the shoulder of a great lion, my friend. I recounted this recurring dream to Samad, and he said the lion represented 'Ali, the son-in-law of the Prophet, whose courage earned him the nickname 'the lion of Islam.' 'Ali was also the root beginning of the Sufi orders which emanated from his teaching.

Over the next few years Abdul Samad was able to travel back to Karachi to see his murshid Sarkar multiple times. In 1976, I was honored to be a witness to Samad's naturalization ceremony—he became an American citizen. He also earned at least one doctorate in those same years, and eventually went to work for one of the Big Three American auto companies. I spent many evenings at his house, discussing practical spirituality, Islam, and listening to *qawwali* records and tapes. A favorite was Nusrat Fateh Ali Khan's 'Lal Shahbazz Qalandar,' which always sent me somewhere else.

Another instance of barely disguised spiritual greed on my part: several of the Sufi orders, especially the Chishti and the Mevlevi (the 'whirling dervishes') sometimes use *sama*, a combination of dance and chant, and if it's appropriate, the attending murshid would allow certain members to go 'out' in a state called *hal*, seeing visions. To no one's surprise, I wanted to experience hal. I still do, and I never have. To my knowledge.

In the summer of 1977, at his urging, Samad and I visited the Lama Foundation in northern New Mexico, where Alpert's *Be Here Now* and Pir Vilayat Khan's *Toward The One* were published. More importantly, Lama is where Samuel Lewis's *maqbara* (grave) sits in a clearing in a pine forest looking over the Rio Grande valley. The Sufis have a custom, *ziyarat*, literally 'tomb visits,' where they visit Sufis of merit. In retrospect, Sam Lewis was the only Murshid in the Chishti Order buried in the United States (that we knew of at the time), and Samad, ever practical, said, "Let's go there." While at Lama, Abdul Samad told me he had been made *Khalifa*, sort of a junior murshid, by Murshid Sarkar. By that time Samad had been initiated into at least four Sufi orders I know of—Chishti, Qadiri, Naqshbandi, and Suhrawardi.

Upon our return, Abdul Samad gave me a Sufi name. Six months later he instructed me to travel again to Lama in the winter months—when visitors were not allowed. I did so, and since the Lama residents remembered my visit there with him, they allowed me to stay at Lama for a while. While there, one of the leaders invited me to live at Lama. It was tempting, especially for someone living in the flat and boring Midwest. However, I was an urban creature, an established computer consultant by that time, and there was no electricity on the mountain at that time. So I regretfully declined. I visited Sam Lewis's grave on that mountainside again and had an unusual experience; I could have found the gravesite with my eyes closed, like knowing where a hot stove is in a cold room. The snow had melted back about 20 feet in all directions. Later that day, looking out over the Rio Grande valley, there was another experience of profound gratitude and melting-of-the-heart.

Back in Detroit, I met some American followers of Hazrat Inayat Khan, (who brought Chishti Sufism to the West in 1911) and later visited the headquarters, Abode of the Message, in New Lebanon, New York. I met Pir Vilayat several times. Oddly, I received more baraka from a dead Sam Lewis than a live Pir Vilayat.

After another visit to Pakistan, Samad said he had, by his murshid's grace, 'graduated' to full murshid status. This meant he could, if he determined it was needed, open his own Chishti circle in the United States. But not all murshids are public, or have a circle. These are called '*mastur*', or hidden.

Wanting to better understand the basis of Sufism, in 1979 and 1980 I studied Arabic for about eighteen months, hoping to eventually read the Qur'an in the original. There is an enormous Mideastern population in the Detroit area, primarily in and around Dearborn. I attended a mosque there for some time, one where the readings and discussions were in English. This did not last. I was as out of place among Qur'an-pounders as I'd have been among Bible-beaters. Samad told me my Arabic sounded Syrian, which made sense, as my instructor was a Syrian.

However, tired of Detroit, desperate for change and more sun, I made plans to leave the Detroit area in early 1982 without Abdul Samad's permission.

About that time, Sarkar passed away. The story Samad told me was that Sarkar was sitting in circle with his followers. He leaned over and whispered to his eldest son, "Time for a change of weather," and died instantly.

Just prior to my departure from Detroit, Samad told me that since I wasn't following the rules (keeping my pants zipped, in this case) I could not play the game, that I should no longer consider myself affiliated with the Chishti-Qadiri orders, and that I should not ask for help from Sam Lewis or Inayat Khan. He did challenge me to find the local spiritual chargeman for the area where I would settle. I took that instruction quite seriously. It eventually led me back full circle to Meher Baba.

My Escape-From-Detroit travels took me around the United States. On the East Coast, I reconnected with Irma Sheppard, my future wife. In late 1982 I traveled to Tucson and was hooked by the scenery and weather. Irma joined me there and we were married by our Rolfer in our back yard in the summer of 1983.

For thirteen years I had no contact with Abdul Samad. He called me in late 1996 and invited me to travel with him to Ajmer, India, home of Khwaja Moinuddin Chishti's tomb-shrine, or dargah. *Khwaja* (master) is the founder of the Chishti Order in India and Pakistan, very high indeed. This invitation led me to believe I had in fact cleaned my heart sufficiently to pass muster with the Sufis. However, wanting to change professions, an exit from the computer industry, I declined the invitation, choosing instead to invest six months in a venture into the film business as a sound effects editor. It was hard, lonely work with long hours, and I decided to take a day off motorcycle riding in the mountains near Taos. Despite being an experienced rider, I crashed the Harley, came back home with a smashed knee, on crutches and oxygen. *Sayonara*, movie industry.

In 2001 Abdul Samad called me in Tucson again, inviting me to India. By that time I was firmly in Meher Baba's hand, so I again declined, not wanting to be a hypocrite, pretending to be a dutiful Muslim Sufi. Heading off to Ajmer alone, Abdul Samad subsequently wrote me a series of God intoxicated letters in which he referred to me by the Sufi name he had bestowed on me years before.

In 2006 Abdul Samad's daughter came through my town, and she had dinner with my wife and myself at our home. She called me

'Uncle Karl,' which made sense, in that her father was my dear brother. The next year, spring of 2007, I traveled back to Michigan in order to bury my father's ashes in the family plot. Now retired, Abdul Samad invited me to his home twice for dinner. He showed me Sarkar's picture for the first time, and indicated he was in regular contact with Sarkar (Sufis consider that the adept may be contacted regardless of time or space). We discussed his last visit to Ajmer, where he stayed with Moinuddin Chishti's own descendants, keepers of the famous dargah, at the heart of the Chishti Order. He told me some amazing stories of staying up all night in the courtyard outside Khwaja's tomb.

Despite all my avoidance of Samad's invitations to Ajmer over the years, in 2010 I was honored to lead *zikr* of over twenty fellow Baba lover pilgrims at the dargah of Khwaja Moinuddin Chishti in Ajmer, Rajasthan, India. Our party, the 2010 Beads On One String Pilgrimage, was led by Don Stevens, at ninety-two the only surviving murid of Murshida Rabia Martin, Hazrat Inayat Khan's first Western disciple. So that amazing circle was closed by Meher Baba's grace.

There has been sporadic email correspondence with Abdul Samad in the past five years. He is now widowed and his children have moved away.

So did that connection, internship, possible muridship, mean anything, do anything? I'd be the last to know. "On the gross plane, but veiled," as the joke goes. While the Sufi path is meant to awaken man to his true nature, it seems to me I gathered a lot of information, little of which has turned into wisdom.

*****

This is the place to fold back time. As already described, Irma joined me in Tucson in early 1983, and we were married by our Rolfer under a *ramada* in our backyard during the first gentle rain of the summer. My parents, an aunt, some Tucson friends, and David and Michael attended, along with their mother.

Irma had already connected with the local Baba group. She had come to Baba in Venice Beach, California, had been to the *saha-vas,* the Los Angeles meetings, and had been to India. We went to the various Tucson Baba parties each year, and when asked about my relationship to Baba, I would usually say I was a 'Baba liker.' Why this resistance to Baba? At that time, though I'd been ostensibly separated from any Sufi connection, Sufism and the Prophet were still my orientation. A poor metaphor was my only response: as a musician, at the time I felt more in harmony with the Prophet Muhammad than Meher Baba.

Irma was collecting what would become an extensive Baba library, and being an omnivorous reader, I was soon reading some of the books as well. I gradually understood the Inayat Khan-Rabia Martin connection, Sam Lewis' connection with them both, and learned about Sufism Reoriented. I found no disagreement between my knowledge of Islam and the Sufi path and the message and role played by Meher Baba. Baba did state that he was the perfect Sufi. That was the tiny opening through which Meher Baba gradually crept into my heart.

It was in the mid-eighties when Irma's daughter, Stephanie, then twenty-one, came to live with us in Tucson. We all continued to socialize with the Tucson Baba community over those years, and I believe they were amused at my continued professed immunity to Meher Baba's charm. I was happy to accompany Irma to several of the Los Angeles sahavases, two camping trips to Meherana, along with two trips to the Myrtle Beach Spiritual Center. All this, convinced that I was just along for the ride.

However, something was happening inside. I had occasional, very clear dreams of Meher Baba. Irma terms vivid dreams such as these 'non-ordinary' and she may be right. I also recall how very important dreams are to the Sufis in the Chishti Order.

Karl Moeller

Dream:
I am rushing, love and lust filled, across town to the House of Love where my woman waits for me. In the house, I rush down a long hallway with many doors on each side. I fling open every single door on both sides of the hallway. Nothing. At the end, I open the door, and instead of my woman, Meher Baba sits in a chair, apparently awaiting me. I drop to my knees and put my head on his feet.

Dream:
I am in a little red Japanese pickup truck with a stick shift. Meher Baba is driving. We're slowly headed up a tree-lined curving street in the hilly, upscale suburb I grew up in. A young woman is walking ahead of us on the sidewalk on the right. Baba slows and indicates to me she needs to hold his hand for just a moment. I stick my head out the window and tell the girl that my 'older brother' thinks she's the cutest thing he ever saw, and that it would make his year if she'd hold his hand. I also tried to convey how harmless we were. She continues to walk, and Baba stays even with her in the truck. Seeing we're not going to give up, she sighs and comes to the truck. I have an image of her hand in Baba's with the dashboard as a backdrop, right in front of me. Baba lets go of her hand, and gives me the 'perfect' sign. She heads back onto the sidewalk. I tell Baba, just before he puts the truck in gear, that I know he's busy running the universe, and that I'd be happy to drive. He smiles, and says, "Driving *is* my job." He puts it in gear and we drive away.

Dream:
Irma and I stand in line for hours in India for darshan with Meher Baba. Just as she was about to get to Baba, the Mandali shout that it's over, Baba is leaving. I rush forward and start arguing with them, to get Irma her tiny time with Baba.

Dream:

Around dusk, I am walking with Meher Baba and my wife, Irma. We are walking in a normal, American suburban street—trees, brick houses. We are walking Irma to her door. After hugs, she heads up her walk to the house and I turn away. 'Karl' has disappeared, and the 'I' is now Meher Baba. 'I' begin to walk back, at one with the trees, the air, all creatures great and small, all around the world. I can feel the entire globe. I am simultaneously walking on this suburban street and am one with the entire planet. My right hip is in agony with every step.

There were other dreams of Meher Baba. This process slogged on from 1983 to 2001, eighteen long, long years. After each dream I'd dismiss it as 'just a dream.' The image of my process that comes to mind is of a tall, tall tree in the forest, which takes decades to fall. Extreme slow motion.

After the last of these dreams, one of those above, Irma asked me, "Does this mean you're a Baba lover in your dreams?" I sheepishly acknowledged it. I could imagine Tucson Baba lovers looking at each other knowingly.

In 2002, on our next visit to the Meher Baba Spiritual Center in Myrtle Beach, South Carolina, we rendezvoused there with daughter Stephanie. Bhau Kalchuri was there on one of his tours of the West, and after Bhau spoke in the Meeting Place, we went up to greet him. He remembered us from Tucson, where he had called me the Piano Man. He asked me if I had been to India. I said no. He slapped me on the shoulder and said, "Come to India!"

I gulped and said, "Yes, sir," before I could even think about it. Irma and Stephanie were utterly delighted! And so we all went. But that's another story of Meher Baba's infinite kindness and grace.

Karl Moeller

*****

It seems arbitrary to cut off the story (stories) just as they get interesting. Another book series is called for—101 Tales AFTER Finding Love.

In 2016, after thirty-three years in the southern Arizona desert, Irma and I, along with our big tabby cat, Sasha, drove and moved across the country to Asheville, North Carolina. We enjoy the large active community of Meher Baba devotees as well as the 'change of weather.' I have written two books of my own thus far, one published historical fiction, the other nonfiction, a layman's look at Sufism, as yet unpublished. I spend some of my time helping Irma, myself, and others turn manuscripts into books, digital Print On Demand, including this one.

I'm still a musician, a keyboardist. I volunteer for some of the many Baba-related projects available here: music, video editing, web maintenance, CD/DVD, poster and book cover graphics, and I am currently on the Asheville Music Sahavas team.

A full life for a weekend hippie.

101 Tales of Finding Love

"REMARKABLE"
—(De-Humorized
and De-Cleverized)

by Alex Morton

Artwork © Claire Mataira

Alex Morton

I used to describe my coming to Baba as 'unremarkable' and now I have given that story line up. I have now realized that this event is now quite 'remarkable' to me and I am writing it with joy.

I have from a young age noticed the absence of authenticity and have not liked it. Maybe it was preverbal, but I don't know that for sure. In retrospect, I know I didn't appreciate Sunday School at my Presbyterian Church and only later realized the concept of lameness was quite prevalent here. After overhearing a discussion between my Mom and Dad regarding the marketing aspects of my attending church at twelve years of age, I realized we were going to church to help my Dad get more people to come to his store. I better understood what I was experiencing at organized religious organizations and how lameness and hypocrisy interacted with each other. I quit going.

Then, I continued my life—and a lot happened. Life was complicated as I seldom knew what was going to happen next! Depending on the alcohol absorption and elimination curves as well as the state of the nervous system of either my Dad or Mom, their responses and behaviors would vary significantly!

In my third year of college, I started searching for what was real, authentic, and meaningful through reading and interacting with other people. Organized religion, especially the Christian churches, offered me very little that I valued and there was no attraction. One night in December 1970, I found myself attending an 'X-mas' party with some older friends in Chapel Hill, North Carolina.

At some point in the evening, I was watching and listening from afar to a vibrant discussion about 'planes of consciousness.' It was a two-against-one discussion and Bob Underwood, whom I had recently met, appeared to be holding his own position quite well, as two other guys were trying to pick apart his beliefs. There were

223

comments such as, "How can you really know what plane of consciousness someone is really on?" These two had obviously different beliefs than Bob had.

After this discussion came to a natural ending, I walked up and said, "Bob! What were y'all talking about?" I asked that question because I had no idea of many of the concepts that were being described and bandied about with such energy. I believe he tried to explain some of these points, but I think it was pointless, as I wasn't 'getting it!' There were too many words that I didn't know!

We continued to chat when he energetically said, "Do you want to get higher than you can get on LSD?"

That was a surprise and I thought that sounded intriguing and said, "Sure! What have you got."

I don't remember exactly how our conversation continued, but it led to the discussion of Meher Baba. Bob said that if I had time around Christmas, I could meet him and some friends at the Meher Spiritual Center in Myrtle Beach, South Carolina. I would get a better idea of what we had been talking about regarding Meher Baba and higher consciousness.

I was going home to Wilmington, North Carolina for Christmas vacation after exams, and the Center was only about sixty-six miles away! "Sure, I'll meet you there." He told me what to bring and the specific time and place to meet. I believe it was a weekend in December 1970 just before or after Christmas.

When I arrived there at the old gateway building, Pine Lodge, the time was about twelve noon and I didn't see Bob's car. I went up to the door, knocked, and was greeted enthusiastically by Kitty Davy with a most welcoming, "Yes! Come in, come in." and I was immediately put at ease. She somehow asked me many more questions than I knew that there were answers to—at least in my head!

I so wish I could remember more about the hour I spent sitting with her, talking about so many things. I have now forgotten the specifics as well as most of the generalities. At that time, I hadn't developed the concept of journaling, so I have nothing written to which I might refer.

I remember repeatedly telling her, "Bob Underwood asked me to meet him here at this specific time." I was clearly more upset than she was that Bob was not yet there. Kitty told me about a group meeting that was about to take place on the Center and that I should attend.

"Run along to the Refectory as it will be starting soon," she said excitedly.

"*Refectory?*" I do remember asking, "*Where* is that?" at least twice, with an appropriate amount of time in between to help mask my cluelessness. I should have been saying, "*What* is that?" as I had never heard this word before.

"Yes!" she repeated. "You will see it. The Refectory is to the right." So I slowly drove down this wonderful tree-lined road, which offered a surrounding comfortable cocoon of green. Arriving at the cabins on the Center, I parked my car, walked up to a building that I hoped was "The Refectory" and walked in.

Inside was a large group, maybe fifteen to eighteen people, sitting around a table, with many more sitting in chairs around the walls. Many were leaning in, staring at a reel-to-reel tape machine and listening to a discussion on similar topics that I had yet to get 'the point' of. Different levels of consciousness, chakras, different kinds of energy were all being discussed on the tape and everyone was transfixed and being silent. So I quickly got transfixed too! I slowly made myself comfortable, adjusting to these tangential topics in my introduction to Meher Baba!

I think someone asked me, "Are you new?" as I perhaps had a semi-lost look on my face. This person showed me the Original

Kitchen where I would be eating and the Studio Room where I would be sleeping and I settled in to wait for Bob to arrive, which he did about three or four hours later. Two other friends were with him.

I stayed two nights, had a pleasant time, despite not really knowing what the Center was all about. I went in the Lagoon Cabin and sat. I don't know if I went to Baba's House or not. I left with many brochures, cards and information from Kitty and drove home to my Dad's house in Wilmington. I was relieved to discover his new girlfriend, Mary C, had known of Meher Baba and the Center too! This made my transition 'back' much easier. We were both excited to share these experiences and discussions about Avatar Meher Baba and established a quick bond with each other!

Recently when I had returned to the Center, I discovered my second visit was on March 27, 1971, just three months after first hearing of Baba. I found myself drawn to frequent trips from Chapel Hill to Baba's 'Home in the West.'

So I continued my life—and a whole lot more happened.

Still, I had this question! "Was Avatar Meher Baba really God?" Over and over I ruminated on this concept. Six years later after being a 'Baba lover' and doing my best to 'follow' Baba, I decided I was going to India, specifically, Meherbad, to ask more questions and get my answers.

I returned after three amazing weeks with an unshakable faith that He was indeed God, not that I understood much more than that! Hearing Eruch's experience of having to interpret and speak Meher Baba's messages, made an indelible impression on me: that Baba said through Eruch, "I am God in human form," and to hear Eruch relating his thoughts, while speaking to massive crowds, saying these words. Eruch expressed, "How can Baba say *THAT*: I am God in human form!" Yet, Eruch continued to have so much love and belief in Baba that he eventually lost those transient doubts.

And then, amazingly, my life continued—and even a whole lot more happened.

I have never lost that conviction that Baba is God, despite the heavy scientific underpinnings of my belief systems, usually requiring demonstrable and observable evidence and proof. Still without 'remarkable' events, visions, or intuitive feelings occurring, I know Baba is God. This faith in Baba being God, the Avatar, is and was self-sealing and steadfast. It doesn't matter to me that I never quickly 'got it' right in following all of his teachings and that I am still 'missing' many of important points about how all this works. I did get the point that I am His.

*****

Alex Morton lives with his best friend, BabaLou, a five-year-old Australian Shepherd girl dog in Brevard, North Carolina in a house bigger than he wants and on five acres of land, bigger and steeper than he now wants. He is a 'kind of retired' psychopharmacologist who currently finds himself working intensely in death penalty trials. He has testified in over eighty criminal trials as an expert witness on the effects of drugs, with the main goal of doing his best in presenting unbiased facts known to him through working with over fifteen thousand patients with major psychiatric disorders in the last forty years. He enjoys long distance endurance runs and now walks. He is a certified InterPlay leader and enjoys acting silly at times. He works hard at being present and is slowly increasing this ability. After writing this story, his next goal is to work more with the difficult concept of "Don't worry. Be Happy"—and accepting Meher Baba's help!

101 Tales
of Finding Love

A HOMECOMING

by Caroline O'Hagan

Central image © Meher Nazar Publications
Framed composition by Karl Moeller

Caroline O'Hagan

I was born in 1946 in England, the third child of four and received instruction in the (Protestant) Christian faith at the village church and at a church primary school I attended from the age of eight to eleven. Once, when I was about five years old, I was sitting on a small ornamental wall in the garden and felt that God was telling me He was real, and that one day I would encounter Him and must remember this message. My secondary school had a Christian ethos but it was rather intellectual in its approach. A devout old priest who taught the confirmation classes proved a source of inspiration, however, and I continued to attend church and Communion for some eight years. Worldly distractions and working with people whose training was scientific then undermined my convictions and I became an atheist, or perhaps an agnostic, because I did not wholly close my mind to God.

I married in 1975 and gave birth to a daughter in 1976 and a son in 1979. We chose a devout Christian couple as godparents to my daughter—at the time I felt intuitively and strongly that I owed her that. After the birth of my second child I felt overwhelmed with my responsibilities as a parent, with reflections on life after death and whether parents and children were reunited in the afterlife (if any). The godparents of my daughter invited me to a Christian evangelist's meeting in southeastern England, where I experienced a sudden conversion and felt that I belonged to Jesus Christ in a personal way.

My husband agreed to attend a lively church with me, and I began going to weekly Bible study and prayer meetings as well as Sunday worship. I received great love, support and fellowship from the church members, but as time went on I was shocked to find the church in general riven by intellectual disagreement.

For example, the English bishops didn't seem know the meaning of God's bidding to change their hearts of stone for ones of flesh, and were determined upon endless dry as dust arguments. I also encountered loveless attitudes to same-gender relationships, no-tably at a local prison Bible class I attended where a vulnerable young gay inmate, on asking for support, was told he could be cured. My marriage ended in divorce after twenty-three years. Gradually my faith weakened and by 2005 I stopped going to church, praying and reading the Bible.

In 2000 I began yoga and was impressed by the philosophy and joyfulness of one of my teachers. When we were relaxing at the end of the class, he told us to float in the 'Ocean of Love,' a very beautiful experience. With his guidance I began to read widely on Yoga, reincarnation, eastern religion, theosophy and so forth, and enrolled in a Yoga teacher training programme. This teacher died very suddenly of heart failure one Christmas, causing me to enroll at the Osho Centre in Pune, where I knew he had studied some twenty years earlier.

I hoped that as he wasn't around to instruct me, I could find out how he had acquired what I valued in him and acquire it too.

I spent three months there during the monsoon of 2007 on the Work as Meditation course. A Gujerati colleague and friend whom I met there kept in touch when I left. He was some three years older than my daughter. I returned to the Osho Centre at Pune twice for short holidays in 2010 and 2014, but during the second of these my Gujerati friend and I decided the place had deteriorated and set off on a tour. He was rather a trusting type of person, and was horrified to be swindled over a hotel bill in Aurangabad. "I know somewhere where no one will cheat us and we can meditate in peace," he stated.

That was how I came to Meherabad for the first time. I knew nothing about Meher Baba before I came—I recall I thought at first the people I met amongst the paths were saying, "Yay Baba!" to me. It was April and very quiet and peaceful. I met Jal Dastoor near Samadhi one day and learned something of Baba and re-ceived some books to read. By the end of ten days I knew I must return.

So I came for four months at the end of the same year and the beginning of 2015 and worked in the tree nursery as a volunteer. Then back to England, where I wound up my yoga teaching practice, explained my plans to my children, mother and siblings, got rid of all my unwanted possessions and let my house. Back to Meherabad for six months in 2015/2016 and again in 2016/2017. Life here isn't all a bed of roses—there have been challenges, illness, injuries. But I have been greatly helped and taught by pilgrims and colleagues. Being able to seek darshan at Baba's Samadhi often is such a privilege. I still feel I have hardly dipped a toe in the Ocean of Love, but even that is so wonderful, so right that at last I feel I have come home.

*****

At this moment I am renting a condo at Meherabad. I have been here since mid-September 2016 and will be leaving March 30, 2017. Then I return to Europe to spend time with my relations in UK and Bordeaux until next September when, Baba willing I return to Meherabad.

101 Tales
of Finding Love

THE ESCORT

by Lindsay O'Keefe

Meher Baba, September 1952
Bindra House, Pune; Photographer: D'Souza

Meher Baba, April 1932, East Challacombe, Devonshire,
U.K. With Delia, Dr. Ghani, Margaret Starr,
Adi Sr., Quentin Todd.

What we are searching for is also searching for us.
The way is to stop.
To let ourselves be found.
Stand still.

In the 1970s, I worked all over the South as a community or-ganizer and was involved with developing federal organic food standards and a wide variety of other sustainable food and land policies. In 1981, after nearly a decade of living in Tennessee, I moved to the Asheville area to settle down. I bought a small farm at the headwaters of a beautiful river in western North Carolina. The idea of making my living from farming was my dream come true.

Every few years, I would fly from North Carolina to visit my par-ents who had retired to California. Following a debilitating stroke, my father had become increasingly odd and withdrawn. When I arrived in California for a visit in late winter 1992, I walked into the kitchen and my father's first words to me were, "You have to buy my car."

I took a step back and asked why. He said the car accident he had six months before was a source of constant argument between him and my mother, and that in particular, she was opposed to his selling the car to a stranger. She feared the car had structural damage, although it had been repaired and the mechanic said it was fine. They had agreed it was not okay to sell it to a stranger, but that I should buy it.

I told Dad I didn't need a car, that I had a little truck which served me well. He appeared not to hear and told me to take it for a drive. I was forty-five at the time and found it ultra strange that my father was pushing me so hard, but on the other hand, his authoritarian ways were familiar. I took the car for a little drive.

The car was nothing special—a white Ford Escort. But for me it was the lap of luxury. It had automatic drive and bucket seats. I had driven thousands of miles over the previous twenty-five years in little vehicles with manual transmissions and flat, uncomfortable boxy seats. Bucket seats were heaven.

I looked at a map and came up with a route for the twenty-five hundred-mile drive home. I decided it could be done in three or four days, and that on the first day I would try to get to somewhere in eastern Arizona. Early one morning after my brief family visit, I set out down the Central Valley in my new little car, feeling peppy and clear. I drove past fields of strawberries, lettuce and cattle, but as I dipped further south, the land became more and more dry. Then, and my memory says it happened rather suddenly, I found myself in the Mohave Desert driving through rain showers. Overhead were dark cloudy skies, the sides of mountains were covered with wildly colored flowers and streaks of green, bathed in shafts of sunlight, surprised by occasional rainbows. It was unimaginably beautiful. Then, just as suddenly, the scene shifted back to dry desert views. I stopped. I thought about turning around to experience that beauty again. Instead, I kept my sights headed east, remembering my duties at home. I stopped at a roadside *tienda* and bought a flat-brimmed Georgia O'Keeffe black leather hat as consolation.

I'm not one to listen to the radio when I drive. I had no CDs. I was alone. As the miles and hours stretched on, I found myself playing a game in my head which went like this: "What would it feel like if I gave up—my business, my best friend, my husband, my child?" Then I would experience and explore the depth and meaning of the feelings that arose. There were few cars on the road, not much that needed tending, and the extraordinariness of this exploration was not lost on me. I cried. I found how unhappy I was, deeply ready for some kind of change, and that surprisingly, the only thing I could not leave was my four-year-old son—and this because our 'agreement,' the contract between a mother and a small child, was different from every other attachment in life. I could not abandon him.

Four days later, I arrived back at my farm at the headwaters of the Green River, energized by some newfound sense of freedom. I fired the woman who helped manage my flower farm, citing the endlessness of unresolved disputes. I spoke with my husband about my unhappiness. Initially, he agreed to marriage counseling, but nothing changed. Ultimately I understood that the role he wanted from me was both best friend and worst enemy—changing from moment to moment—his choice. We decided to divorce but over a period of two years, we were unable to come up with a property settlement. We had a farm. I had a successful business. I employed eight people and supplied sixty garden centers in several states. He wanted me to keep supporting him.

During this period of time trying to negotiate a 'reasonable' end to my marriage, I developed an almost continuous vertigo. It was profound and limiting—something worse than unending confusion because it had such a strong physical edge. I had difficulty finding myself in space. Ultimately, it was also liberating—I felt I might die or at least get some autoimmune disease, and I needed to complete my new direction.

One day, in the midst of this exhausting stalemate, I found myself driving on the Blue Ridge Parkway (which is a National Park). I heard my mind say, "All this is mine and none of this is mine." I made the decision to let go of the farm and the business. I went to see a bankruptcy lawyer. I crunched the numbers: the assets of farm and business offset the debts so that I could walk away with a clean slate. I gave the lawyer a go ahead to file papers in the federal court in Charlotte.

I relaxed a bit, although the vertigo continued. I remembered that I was capable of making big decisions without allowing myself to grieve, so I decided to go on retreat before the filing of the bankruptcy to 'feel my feelings.' I was letting go of my life's dream. For some reason, I knew the retreat had to be by the ocean, even though I hated the ocean. The ocean was deep and menacing and filled with sharks. Whatever. My mind was clear and time was short—how could I find a retreat center by the ocean?

I had a friend who had been going to a retreat center in Myrtle Beach for fifteen years, and I called her to learn more about it. She never mentioned Meher Baba. She was not interested in Meher Baba. The place she went was filled with interesting and friendly people, poets and hippies it seemed. It was by the ocean. It was cheap and safe for her and her young daughter. She gave me a phone number. I called, and they said I could FAX a letter explaining that I was a spiritual seeker (true—I'd had a mindfulness practice for thirty years and a degree in Asian studies; I loved God and secretly had conversations with Him since childhood). And that I hadn't used drugs in six months (also true). They FAXed back and said, "Come." No Universal Message or other identifying information. I arrived a week or so later.

It was October of 1996. I'd had a computer for several months, but I found the probable learning curve daunting, so I put a funny hat on the computer and never turned it on. I don't know if one could have searched for The Meher Spiritual Center on the internet in those days, but in my mind I was going to the Meier Center or Some Kind of Spiritual Center (maybe Jewish? Somebody named Meier.) It didn't matter to me. It was a retreat center by the necessary but foreboding ocean. It was cheap. It was safe for me and my young son. I needed to go 'feel my feelings' about leaving everything to the federal court in Charlotte.

So, on a very beautiful fall day, I drove with my eight-year-old son from my about-to-be-abandoned mountain home to Savannah, Georgia in my boxy-seated little truck to deliver a small order of flowers to a garden center. Then, on to the 'Meier' Center in Myrtle Beach. I arrived sometime after 11 p.m. to be greeted by three patient, very polite people in a rustic building called The Gateway. They explained that I was arriving past curfew, but that it was okay. The tall man named Walter would show me to my cabin. I followed Walter's vehicle through a dense dark forest. We stopped. I could hear ocean waves in the near distance. It was lovely. Walter set our suitcase on the steps and said, "This is Cove 2 and if you need anything, I'll be in the Caretaker's Cabin." I wondered what that meant. I knew his intention was to let me know I was not alone, but I had no idea what or where this Care-taker's Cabin might be. I decided I would think about it tomor-row. I was tired.

My son, Noah, and I stepped into the cabin. Two little beds pushed up against wood paneled walls. A bathroom, a little kitchen. But, oh no! Photos on the walls of some unknown Indian Guru. In 1970 I had traveled overland alone to India seeking to move to Tibet, and while there had made a firm decision to NEVER go anywhere near an Indian guru. Ugh! But I was tired, and I decided I would find out more, *tomorrow*. Why had my friend not told me this was some kind of ashram? But no, face this tomorrow.

What happened of course, is that there was no tomorrow. Time stopped. There was instead, a shift in my universe. My life changed forever. Instead.

I fixed the sheets and blankets on my bed and Noah's and fell quickly asleep, listening to the steady pounding of waves in the distance. After sleeping for several hours, I awoke transfixed in stillness. My body was there, but it could not move. I was bathed in Meher Baba's glance. I was held in His embrace. There was no distance, there was nothing but Him. It was not a dream. He was there, clear as day, beautiful, so very beautiful. More Real than anything I had known before. I knew love for the first time ever.

I stayed still, knowing that I could stay in this moment of love, knowing that to move would awaken my body in the old way, or so I thought. I waited and did nothing. Eventually, things shifted back into a normal sense of 'I' and an awareness of time. I no-ticed the sun rising. The moment had passed in which I was be-yond any experience of time. It was over, and it was permanently present. I looked out a window and had the thought, "I'll just step outside and clear my head."

Behind the cabin I found a little bench. I sat down there, took a breath intending to become more mindful, but instead of 'clearing my mind,' I became overwhelmed and infused with the scent of fabulous flowers, something like gardenias and roses. It was October, there were no flowers. The scent took my breath away. And in that moment I completely got it that my life was no longer my own, that I was no longer alone.

And even though I was certain of this, and grateful beyond gratitude, I listened as some small part of me showed anger. I had a rule. Here was this direct experience of Truth, and dammit, some kind of Indian guru. The part of me whose job it was to protect me from spiritual charlatans was not happy at all, and the internal chatter began.

I did not buy into the chatter, nor could I push it away. Both internal situations were present: one Real and one, given my history, reasonable. I thought to myself, "What is the next thing to do?" I decided to try to find another human being, someone who might help me orient to the Center.

So, with time, I wandered over to the Original Kitchen and found someone named Arthur sweeping and cleaning. He seemed gentle enough with a colorful little handkerchief on his head. I said to him, "Why can't I wear sandals here?" The FAXed letter which invited me to Meher Center had given no heads-up about rules or about Meher Baba, and it seemed safer to start my investigation with a question about rules. I didn't have shoes other than sandals with me, and it pleased my angry part to push a little on whether I could bend this rule. Arthur told me about snakes on the paths and the anger dissipated some. Then I asked, "Why can't I use the *I Ching* here?" (I had brought three translations of the *I Ching* with me, a book I had discovered as a teen, and my plan had been to consult them as I 'felt my feelings' about the upcoming bankruptcy.) Arthur responded that Meher Baba had said that the *I Ching*, like astrology, was good spiritual science, but that most who used these esoteric systems did not understand them. That if I wanted to know more, there was a library somewhere near my cabin and I could read what He had said. Again, my angry part relaxed, and I found myself getting very curious.

I went through that day in a happy fog. There was a tour: I walked the grounds with a lovely woman named Marty, who had joy in her as she told stories of a young Meher Baba kissed by a saint, pounding his head on a stone in his room for months, trying to come back down to this reality. I thought of my own vertigo. I learned of two women who found and built this ashram at the end of World War II, and their meticulous and loving attention to every detail and every person who came seeking. I went into buildings that were sacred sites of gatherings, and although I could not understand these things, I did sense sanctity in the atmosphere. My son, Noah, came back from a short outing near our cabin and reported he had been walking with a man in a long white robe, and I thought, "He has been with Him, too." And I breathed in the wonder again.

I told no one of my experience during that first night, yet somehow I wanted to make a report on this to see what The Other (whomever) might say. At the Gateway, they had given me a little piece of paper with the name of my Contact at the Center. Someone named Marshall Hay. I went to a program that night, and there was Marshall annotating a silent film about Baba and some of His followers. I asked Marshall to come over to the kitchen and have tea with me after the film. I told him of my experience. He listened carefully and said nothing, as though this was the most normal thing in the world. He suggested that I come to a tea the next afternoon to meet his fiancée, Mimi. He thought we would enjoy meeting. I also met my future husband Dennis that first weekend, although we would not realize our connection for several years.

There was a sweetness and a cadence to all these events at the Center. Like it was just there, waiting—waiting the way I had waited to stay within Baba's embrace. I knew that my mind, trained in the texts and histories of Asia, was going to try to reframe this experience. I made a decision to come back to the

Center once a month for a year, to keep myself from over-thinking all this. To let it settle in and be whatever it was.

I went back to the bureaucracy of my old life. Papers were filed with the federal court in Charlotte. Two weeks later I gave up everything: acreage, greenhouses, a home, cars, clothing, pictures on the walls, a business that was grossing over $200,000 a year. Everything. The federal court gave me back $7,000 of my stuff: pots and pans and clothes and the white Ford Escort. Everything else went into limbo.

A month after my first visit, I drove back to the Center in my little white Ford Escort. You remember—the one that my father said I had to buy, the one with the bucket seats, the one in which I'd imagined giving up everything. At the Gateway, the car died. Someone suggested a mechanic named Billy, a native of Myrtle Beach who had met Baba. Billy assured me he could fix it. A week later, Billy called and said he could not for the life of him figure out the problem and referred the car on to another mechanic. And then another. No one was able to diagnose the problem. The car was junked in Myrtle Beach.

I bought a ticket and rode the bus back home to North Carolina. I thought about the journey from my father in California to my Real Father. The cross-country trip in the little white car, the realization that I could let almost everything go. Once I began the process of letting go, there was no turning back. The vertigo began when I tried to negotiate rationally with my former husband. Then a moment of clarity: "All this is mine, and none is mine." Somehow, all this leading to a rendezvous with Baba, the One who could hold me as no other.

A month later, a second visit. The death of the little white Ford Escort at the Gateway. As though there needed to be punctuation, a period at the end of the story. Maybe an exclamation point. After giving up 'everything,' there would always be one more thing I hadn't noticed I could let go. The Ford Escort (don't you love the name—I had an *escort*!) was the one possession of

245

material value I had kept from the bankruptcy, and it too had to go! Letting go of the mind, the will to control. Becoming His.

I was able to visit the Center once a month that first year. It was grounding to see the Center through its seasons, to make myself at home there. I had no money. Sometimes I had enough for the trip down, but not enough to get home. People helped me—I never asked. I read *God Speaks* on that second visit—waiting for the Escort to be repaired, I had plenty of time. I thought I understood every word. I've read it four times since, and each time it is as though I have never read it before. And at night, and every night for twenty years, when I lie down to sleep I snuggle in with Baba, and although it is not as it was that first time of realizing Him, I know that He is with me and that I am not alone.

*****

Lindsay lives with her husband of fourteen years, Dennis O'Keefe, at the confluence of three mountain streams twenty-five miles north of Asheville, North Carolina. Her son, Noah, lives in Anchorage, Alaska. She is a psychotherapist in private practice in Asheville.

101 Tales of Finding Love

AN AGNOSTIC TURNED MEHER BABA LOVER:
An Endless Journey of Love

by S Narendra Prasad

Manzil-e-Meem, Mumbai, 2012

Sahavas procession—Puri September 2016

Narendra Prasad at the entrance to the
mini-Taj Mahal, Beads On One String
pilgrimage, Maharastra, 2010

Photo by Karl Moeller

B
ACKDROP:

Why does God take so many incarnations? Why are there three million Gods in the Indian folklore? Are Rama and Krishna mere mythical figures or not? Does God really take human form? Would I ever get a chance to believe that God in human form exists?

These and more were some of my baffling questions, which bothered me as a teenager. I did not seek any answer or explanation from my parents, for I believed that these concepts are perhaps mythical and had no basis in reality! These were my private thoughts and I did not seek any explanation. Although my father was a very devout spiritual person, I never ventured into seeking answers from him. Reading scriptures and Bible for answers was not even attempted as they seemed very arcane and beyond my understanding!

INITIAL YEARS:

Even before these questions arose, my mother used to tell me—when I was a ten- or eleven-year-old—that I was blessed by Meher Baba, none other than God Himself. This had happened in the famous 1953 Andhra tour [1] in Tadepalligudem, where my father was working as a teacher. My mother took darshan of Baba, while I was in her womb as a five-month-old foetus! Looking back, whenever Baba lover friends enquire whether I took Baba's darshan, I reply that while I did not see Baba, Baba had seen me ! I used to read, as a young boy, the Telugu monthly publication, *Avatar Meher,* but could not fathom Baba's saying, "I have come not to teach, but to awaken." It was beyond my grasp—when He was silent, how could one be awakened?!

While I remained an agnostic for a long time, little did I know that my college education and place of stay were important land marks for the Baba world as He gave public darshan in Sir CR Reddy college, Eluru [2] (my Alma mater) and my two-year stay itself was in Katta Subba Rao garden, where Baba stayed.

The answers for my questions came in a very unsuspecting way some three decades later, from Baba.

Dehra Dun New Life Property:

I was employed in Dehra Dun, in the north of India, as a scientist in the field of Ecology. Interestingly, one of this discipline's chief principles is that every living thing is connected with everything else in a unified whole—close to a saying of Baba's, reflecting "we all are one"! My reintroduction to Baba was by way of attending the annual sahavas of Baba in Dehra Dun in March 1996. To me, the sahavas was a totally new experience and I was much impressed with the sincerity, care and devotion of the Baba lovers, led by Dr. G.S.N. Murthy [3], known popularly as a talkative disciple of the silent master! I started poring over Baba's literature such as Jean Adriel's *Avatar*, the *Discourses, God Speaks* and others.

This opened a whole new perspective for me, hitherto unsuspected and least imagined. In the process, I literally stopped working for three months and felt deeply of His love. It was of course, a eureka moment for me!! I felt like shouting from roof tops about the most wonderful phenomenon called Meher Baba!! It made tremendous sense and gave a lot of answers to my questions.

I visited Meherabad in July 1998 for the first time on the occasion of Silence Day.

The moment I stepped onto the threshold of the tomb shrine, tears burst forth like torrents and I was sobbing beyond control for hours and days! Indeed, I was overwhelmed with the experience and found that my world revolved around Baba and Baba alone. Baba further drew me into His love orbit in a very unique fashion in 1998 by involving me in acquiring a part of the New

Life property including the small hut at Manjri Mafi where He and the women companions stayed from January to April 1950.[4] Baba wanted to dispose of the property to a chosen group of four of his lovers from Delhi in May 1950. However, when this group expressed their inability to buy the property, Baba was annoyed [5] and declared that this property would then go to an 'outsider.' For fifty years this property was out of bounds to Baba lovers who wanted to visit the premises, including Baba's room and women companions' rooms.

In 1998 August, our family moved to the Indian Institute of Petroleum staff quarters, which is less than a kilometre from the New life property. I often used to visit Mrs. Subhadra, wife of Shatrughna Kumar, and she would narrate her experiences of Baba and the companions during New life. On one fateful day in September/October 1998, she suddenly asked me to try and acquire the property so that Baba lovers would be able to take darshan of the sacred room, where Baba stayed. She explained how sad it was to see Baba lovers being turned away from darshan on important days such as the 24 March anniversary sahavas programme at Manjri Mafi. Initially I was apprehensive about the entire project, but as Baba would have it, within a few months, I found myself deeply involved in the task of securing the precious premises.

I contacted Bhau Kalchuri, Eruch Jessawala and many others across the country for possible help. The best advice I got from Eruch was, "If you are sincere, Baba will help."[6] Surely, it did work with lots of setbacks, hopes and help. The process involved setting up a new legal entity—a registered society named as "Avatar Meher Baba New Life Charitable Trust," for not only raising funds to acquire the Baba hut along with additional surrounding land, but also try and promote the New life principles of how to seek God.

To cut short a long story, by His grace, the premises were legally secured on 12 January 2000, precisely on the fiftieth anniversary of His and His New Life companions' arrival in Dehra Dun. This process of acquisition was so intense and I found myself veering from despair to bright hopes, so I felt I was in a pressure cooker state designed exclusively by Baba for reasons best known to Him. This experience to me was an opportunity that Beloved Baba provided me to constantly remember Him and leave all worries to Him, and not to bother too much about the results.

Baba lovers in Dehra Dun, who apparently had tried earlier to secure the acquisition, told me that the securing of the New life property is nothing short of a miracle! As the structure was found to be vulnerable, all the trustees decided on measures to protect it. After deliberating on various possibilities, an overhead concrete encasement was built over the hut. All major events such as Baba's birthday, His arrival in Dehra Dun and the New Life are celebrated in a new hall constructed to seat around five hundred persons. Free medical consultancy is being offered at the premises.

Yet again in 2003, Baba gave me another opportunity to help organize a golden jubilee celebration of His Golden Jubilee darshan anniversary of 1953 at Dehra Dun. It was a unique opportunity in several ways. The two-day event was held at 101 Rajpur Road, the very same location where Baba gave public darshan in December 1953, and where Baba used to visit the mandali. It was the very same place where Baba gave the Master's Prayer too. More than five hundred persons attended the sahavas from far away places in India.

Following the sahavas, in order to spread Beloved's message of love and truth, it was decided by five or six Baba lovers from Dehra Dun and Roorkee to hold a sahavas in fifty different places associated with Baba's ministry. Again I was fortunate enough to be associated with this project for about three months.

SAHAVAS IN BABA PLACES:

Thus the Golden jubilee event heralded a new phase of Baba work to hold sahavases in places connected with His universal work. It so happened that we could travel to twenty-five different places sanctified by Baba in the erstwhile Uttar Pradesh (now Uttara Khand), and Himachal Pradesh. For example, these places include Haridwar, Rishikesh, various places associated with Baba in Dehra Dun itself, Shimla, Kullu, and other places. While it was wonderful to discover that some of the buildings where Baba stayed still exist, more importantly it dawned on me that people have a very high degree of receptivity of Baba's messages of love and truth.

At this point of time, Baba in quick succession made two major changes to my health condition and to my professional activity. I had to be hospitalized for a major health problem, followed by my professional relocation to Hyderabad from Dehra Dun. In both of these concerns, there was the palpable strong support of Beloved Baba, which again fortified my experience of His limitless love! I'm extremely fortunate that my professional travels, to a very substantial degree, have inextricably been linked with His work. Thus invariably, I will be in one or another place where Baba had visited during His extensive travels. It was such a great pleasure to reconnect with the places sanctified by Baba. I thought that perhaps a great value could exist for a large number of Baba lovers as well to reconnect with these places and get an opportunity to make some lucky souls hear about Meher Baba.

Thus the very first initiative in the 2010 Banaras sahavas was a unique event, wherein more than five hundred Baba lovers participated. Coincidentally, this was the year I participated, on the invitation of Don Stevens, in the 'Beads on One String' programme in India. A procession was also held from Sarnath to Varanasi, commemorating Baba's New Life journey on foot from Sarnath.[7]

Over the years, such *sahavases* were held in Mumbai to commemorate His stays in Manzil-e-Meem, Uttarkashi, Surat, Kashmir, Puri, Ranchi, Kolkata, Goa, and Andhra. This activity has now been formalized under the aegis of "Endless Journey of Love," with seven trustees and supporting education activities in places where the sahavas is held and in other places needing such support.

In retrospect, I'm most fortunate that Baba's nazar was on me constantly to enable me to enter His love orbit. I hope this will continue till the endless end!

*****

I live in Hyderabad, an important place for Meher Baba's Manonash phase of work in the New life. I do voluntary work for an organization in Hyderabad spearheading the free software movement and also as an expert for conducting environmental appraisals. In between, I visit Meherabad three, four or more times in a year.

References
1.
http://www.lordmeher.org/rev/index.jsp?pageBase=page.jsp&nextPage=3248 DOI 29 Apr2017
2
http://www.lordmeher.org/rev/index.jsp?pageBase=page.jsp&nextPage=3258 DOI 29 Apr2017
3
http://www.lordmeher.org/rev/index.jsp?pageBase=page.jsp&nextPage=5440 DOI 29 Apr2017
4
http://www.lordmeher.org/rev/index.jsp?pageBase=page.jsp&nextPage=2865 DOI 29 Apr2017

5 Keki Desai-unpublised hand written dairy, 98 pages

6 Love street lamp post , October 2001, page 23
7
http://www.lordmeher.org/rev/index.jsp?pageBase=page.jsp&nextPage=2843 DOI 29Apr2017

101 Tales of Finding Love

BABA'S GIFTS TO ME

by Bishka Ravenel

Meher Baba and Dr. El Pusser

When I was a child, I was drawn to the mysteries of life. I was always in awe of the beauty of nature. I also was the one who would always ask 'why' in regard to people acting a certain way or in response to the harshness of the world events. My childhood friend, Judy and I thought adults to be rather strange. We were given free play of the imagination and creativity. Often, we had difficulty following rules, and although we did not get into serious trouble, we were viewed as the 'mischievous ones.' Nonetheless, although we were rascals with independent minds, we shared this unspoken reverence for life marked by honoring all creatures, admiring the beauty of nature, feeling such excitement in the act of discovery, and recognizing the kindness in others. These qualities were Baba's gifts to me, helping to prepare me to come to Baba years later.

I remember crying over the films like "King of Kings," and "The Robe." I felt an indescribable peace and love while watching the portrayal of the life of Christ. I also felt these feelings in nature and sitting next to the organ as my mother, the church organist, played. Being a sensitive child, I felt the suffering of others. The world was hard for me to understand. I remember looking up into the sky and feeling such love for God. For me, it was not a man in the sky, but an essence, a feeling of deep love. These feelings were Baba's gifts to me and my soul sister, Judy.

Baba had given to me the gift of search, longing to know myself and to understand my experience. I was moved by 'the sound of a different drum' and that was obvious. Being the odd one in my family, I was not truly moved by traditional aims. To think of just getting married and having children I would think, "Is that all there is?" Although I did feel great love for my family, they did not understand me very well. I had deep questions about life, including why I had dreams of Nazi Germany, being chased by soldiers, dreams of fire, fear. Being born in the fifties, the war well over, I did not have a framework of meaning to understand my experience. I became insecure, filled with anxiety. I did read in one volume of *Lord Meher* where Baba said that many who died in the camps in WWII would reincarnate in the United States their next lifetime. My teenage years were difficult. I recall a memory of going to the YMCA with my parents, as they were very active. I was taken into a steam bath, and the steam coming out of the pipe triggered fear. It was not until years later that I could process this as a memory of the gas chambers in Germany.

I felt this deep sense of love for God on the one hand, and tremendous anxiety on the other. I longed to make sense of my life. I developed panic attacks and felt alienated. This was also Baba's gift to me, for in my desperation, I knew there had to be an answer, a way, a door to help me. It was not the church for me, nor was it the psychiatrist, as that avenue was tried as well. I was blessed by having Judy in my world, for we understood one another and would retreat to the woods, mirroring a peace we both played out through creative acts of imagination and discovery.

I had this conscious desire at eighteen, to move to a larger city, Minneapolis, to meet people from other cultures, and so I did. I lived in a boarding house and worked a year at the Swedish Hospital, which my great-grandfather from Sweden founded in 1902. I was to attend nursing school the following year. While working as a nursing aide, I met people from all over the world. At nineteen, I met an orderly, Frank, who wore a turban. Frank was in his twenties then and carried this inner light and was filled with this love I was drawn to. He was a Sikh and his master was Charan Singh. Although his culture was foreign to me in most ways, I was so moved by his loving presence. He invited me to attend their satsangs and he gave me a book called *Light on Sant Mat*. When I started to read this book, the philosophy made sense to me. It spoke of reincarnation, purifying the self and the path to God Realization.

My encounter with this man and my orientation to this perspective in life was the first experience I had this lifetime that helped relieve some of my inner confusion. I was able to understand some of my deeper longings and to place my dreams of Nazi

Germany into a meaningful framework. I felt a peace around the Sikhs and although I did not join their order, I remained a friend and was so grateful for knowing them. In my twenties, I entered nursing school and counseling to get help with some of my anxieties and to understand and work with wounds from childhood. I began for the first time to feel an improved sense of worth. These experiences were Baba's gifts to me, to be able to know I was on a path to transform myself and the discovery that there were other individuals in this world who felt as deeply as I did about following the path of the heart. What I mean by this, is that it was monumental for me to meet others who placed the love of God first as a foundation of being, living in everyday life. I no longer considered myself such a misfit in this world.

There were more mentors and beautiful souls who came into my life. I was so fortunate to have met Dr. Kubler-Ross in my Oncology rotation at the University of Minnesota in the 1970s. She is the author of the original *Death and Dying*. Her whole life's work entailed introducing the practical applications of preserving the dignity of dying into health care systems. Her compassion in serving others mirrored that depth of love for others within me. Her wisdom, her spirit and selflessness inspired me to supervise a nursing home a couple of years following nursing school. I also gave talks to high schools on thanatology. Not only did I assure in my work in Gerontology that no one died alone, but this work also brought to light my inner examination of how I felt about death. These experiences were Baba's gifts to me. My nursing practice itself became my greatest teacher. There came another Sikh of a different order, whom I worked with. We would spend hours talking about life, death, God and suffering, from what I considered to be a worldview that again, made more sense to me than my Western upbringing. This man was another gift in my experience, mentor and friend.

In my late twenties, I moved to the mountains of Asheville North Carolina. I became so alive marked by the tremendous beauty that surrounded me, adventure with hiking, water, nature, along with meeting people of like mind. My inner search and development continued. I attended Rev. Chad O'Shea's Unity church. I attended many seminars pertaining to the healing arts, women's growth, wellness and alternative medicine. I worked with disabled children as a registered nurse and attended school, earning a degree in philosophy at the University of North Carolina at Asheville.

Studying the Socratics, Eastern Philosophies, Plato, Ralph Waldo Emerson and others enhanced my sense of growth. I related to what I was studying from within. I studied the world religions and felt a beauty and commonality at their core ideologies. Such pursuits expanded my awareness, knowledge and understanding. I viewed life from a total perspective and the study of various Theosophies exhilarated my being. I felt this driving force of healing within me—an opening, a blossoming. I was evolving. Although I still had work to do on myself to transform many insecurities, I again continued in counseling for the support to move in growth. At times, I felt such inner joy associated with my love for God.

At the end of 1981, I met a most unusual man, Dr. El Pusser. He worked in staff development at the facility for the disabled where I was a staff nurse. One day, I walked into his office and asked, "What do you do in here?" I had never met this man before as I was new to the facility. What did I see he was doing?! He was viewing an animated filmstrip of "Plato's Analogy of the Cave." Wow! I studied this in Philosophy. This analogy represents the darkness we go through in ignorance, shackled to the wall of maya. There is an opening, a light at the entrance and other souls who are freed from maya enter the cave and assist others to be unshackled. This is the analogy of the journey of the soul back to Self-understanding. A kindred spirit I discovered by meeting this man. I was excited and felt I knew him from another time. We shared on such deep level, became friends.

Little did I know at that meeting, that Dr. El was to be my link to Meher Baba. El was, to me, androgynous in some ways. He was strong, but had feminine characteristics too such as warmth, nurturance, and he expressed his feelings so well. I felt I could talk with him about anything, just like one of my girlfriends—I was not used to a male with this type of balance. I had challenges with trust issues with men from my childhood wounds. Hence, El was a man I could trust. Knowing him became my healing with male issues of mistrust. Meeting this unusual man, Dr. El, was Baba's gift to me—my life was never the same after meeting him. We would talk for hours and go on walks in nature, often silent.

One day, he brought me a book called *Beams from Meher Baba on the Spiritual Panorama*. He also showed me Baba's picture and I thought to myself, "Why does El look so much like Him?" From then on, when I would see Baba's picture, I would think of El. Little did I know Baba was up to something here. I did not have the concept of Avatar in my understanding until I read about this in Baba's writings. A part of my conditioning, growing up Christian, was challenged.

Reading Baba's works however, made so much sense to my heart. I had always intuited and viewed life from a total view. I was not grounded in linear thinking. This is why Emerson's Oversoul made so much sense to me, placing life from the view of the journey of the soul as a purpose for human life. Although El was ten years my senior, age mattered not to this deep compatibility, in which both of us were not grounded in Western thought. He was a mirror of the deepest part of my experience.

One day, El asked me if I would be interested in going to Myrtle Beach to Baba's Home in the West. I said sure. This was another gift in my life from Baba, as this journey to the Center changed my life. The Center was absolutely beautiful. I stayed in the women's bungalow filled with anticipation and slight apprehension. I was not in my mind going to join anything. I felt at that time, I was not going to join anything that advocated exclusivity or narrow perspectives. I was in for a remarkable surprise at Baba's Home in the West.

I loved being at the Center. I felt this pure energy, excitement accompanied by an eager inquisition. I met Jane Haynes, Kitty Davy, Jeff Wolverton and so many more beautiful souls! Much of my time was spent reading Baba's words, walking on the beautiful grounds, swimming in Baba's ocean and interacting with others. Here was a being who declared Himself to be God, and although I had some reservation about 'Avatar,' after absorbing myself in studying the writings of Baba, a divine revelation came over me. I felt from the depths of my being that Meher Baba declared the entire meaning of human existence IN THE MOST PERFECT WAY. I knew He was who He claimed to be! Not only did I know this from within me, but I intuited I had known Him in another time. Baba's greatest gift to me was the removal of my veils to recognize Him as the Avatar. I decided I wanted to live by the Center, and in the summer of 1983, accepted a position at a small town hospital in Southport, North Carolina, which happened to be located forty-five minutes from the Meher Spiritual Center—another gift from Baba.

Dr. El, who was working through challenging times, remained in North Carolina. For the next year, I worked at this small hospital, lived alone on the Intercoastal Waterway, and visited the Center as often as I could. No longer were there days of looking at Baba's picture and thinking of El—now I looked at a picture of El and I thought of Baba. It was as if Baba had stolen my heart. I will never forget summer days at Baba's home. I would swim at Baba's warm beach—glistening bright, magical blue. I often visited Jane, Kitty, Happy Club, and others. I so enjoyed this gift of being close to the Center. I did not see El for some time, although we kept up with correspondence.

I will never forget that summer. What took place within me was another gift from Baba. I had been in counseling aiming at the healing of the relationship between my father and me. Like a 'thief in the night,' Baba shifted my emotional pain. I let go of this age-old feeling of rejection from my father and felt reliance upon Meher Baba as my father. I forgave my father, myself and other members of my family. For the first time in my life, I felt like a huge weight was lifted from me. No longer feeling this rejection as I once did, I began to feel such love and compassion for my father. I felt reliance upon Baba for my strength. I felt naked, free of attachment to unfulfilled needs not met as a child, but this was accompanied by feelings of love and freedom. Baba helped me release old wounds of my heart. This was His gift to me. I was never the same person. I felt reborn—new and grateful that a part of my ego that had carried emotional pain had died.

I moved back to the mountains of North Carolina at the closing of 1984. I often thought of Dr. El, but had not heard from him for some time. I attended Unity Church, taught Sunday school, and worked at a local hospital. I told Rev. Chad at Unity about my experience of being introduced to a Perfect Master. Chad ordered some of Baba's books for the library at the church. My relationship with Baba continued to grow, now such an important part of my world. I was so grateful to El for being my link to Baba. His friendship in my life truly became very valuable to me. In 1986, I received a letter from El. He had been through many life changes, including a divorce.

Fast forwarding my story—El and I were married the following year on December 3rd, 1987. Our lives were centered on Baba. Although there were many challenging times, there existed a solid foundation of love, with both of us serving the Master, Meher Baba. El brought three most beautiful children into my world. My relationship to them meant so much to my heart and does to this day. Living with El was like living with my best friend. He loved Meher Baba so very much. Being a mystic, he brought much joy to my life, including spontaneity, a childlike nature, and a knowing that anything was possible with enough love and Baba directing our lives.

We relocated to Nashville, Tennessee at the closing of 1992. I attended Vanderbilt Divinity School until December 1995. We met such beautiful Baba friends, including Bill and Peggy Stephens and Jamie Newell and his wife. Weekly, we so enjoyed attending the meeting at the Stephens' home. Such friends in Baba were our gift.

In December 1995, we relocated to Charleston, South Carolina where I accepted a position at the Medical University of South Carolina. We lived on Folly beach, which was absolutely beautiful. For the next several years, we traveled to the Center often and attended Baba meetings, often holding meetings at our home on Folly Beach. The wonderful Baba friends we met in Charleston became our dearest friends. I became close to Jane Haynes and would at times drive her to Mepkin Abbey where she visited the Monks. I considered Jane to be my spiritual mother. We bought a second home in the mountains of North Carolina. This lovely cabin's ceiling was designed after the ceiling in the library on the Center. It was pyramidal in design and one could not keep from thinking of the Center while looking at it. This second home was formerly owned by Bill and Peggy Stephens. Twice a month, El and I would venture to this home and so enjoyed not only the mountains, but also the energy of Baba emanating in this sacred home.

El became ill in 2001 and required Cardiac Bypass surgery. Although he recovered fairly well for a time, he developed an Aortic Abdominal Aneurysm. This entailed extensive surgery and our lives changed dramatically. Home health was needed for a time. Convalescence was a major endeavor. After a few months, El seemed to be improving.

In December of 2002, I had an opportunity to travel to Baba's home in India. I had not been to India this lifetime, yet arriving in Mumbai, I felt the smells were so familiar. My trip to India was absolutely phenomenal, but this would be another story. It was more than words can express, and was Baba's precious gift to me. Being at Baba's home where the Avatar walked, and meeting the most Divine Souls of His circle, touched my heart so deeply. I laid my head on Baba's Tomb and talked with Baba about my concern for El's well-being. I wanted to be there for El in the highest way of love, as his health was not good. In my absence, El had taken his new acquaintance, Alexander Ravenel to the Center. Alexander watched over El while I was in India. El and Alexander shared a deep respect and love for one another. They spent hours talking about life and the spiritual path. El introduced Alexander to Meher Baba. To this day, Alexander refers to Dr. El as his mentor who helped him advance spiritually.

I returned from India at the end of December to find El in the hospital. As always, it was so good to see him and actually, he looked quite radiant. El had the challenge of balancing his moods in life, often marked by hospitalizations for stabilization. Due to the impact of his physical decline, he became vulnerable to instability. Hence, I will never forget that visit to the hospital after my return from India. The beauty of his essence was present, as if in that moment, we again shared this deep love and connection. Nothing else mattered. Nothing, no matter what transpired, he and I always simply resumed that beautiful depth of love when together. A Baba lover once told me that when you visit Baba's Tomb, your path and those connected to you will advance.

Five days after I returned from India, El wrote emails which I have today, in which he thanked everyone in his life. He thanked me for loving him and sharing his difficult path, and he thanked his children and others for their love. This was on a Saturday, I believe. On January 6th, a week after my return from India, I called El as I always did when I was at work. There was no answer. When I returned home in the afternoon, there was no answer at the door. When I walked into our home, I found that El had passed away.

Unless one has experienced this, I think no one would know the degree to which one has to suddenly shift and cope. Of course the police had to be called, the coroner. First, however, I called my precious Baba friends, who came to me within minutes. Regardless of the police being present, five of my dearest Baba friends and I said the Master's Prayer over El's body. My beloved El, my divine companion in Baba, had left while I was at work that day. I will never forget the comfort of the Baba friends with me those moments of my life. Their presence gave me strength. They loved El so much too. All of this experience has been Baba's gift to me. Death of a close one is a teacher, and I will say to you, that after seventeen years of marriage with a foundation of loving the Avatar, this was the hardest experience in my life. I was a widow in my late forties and I had lost my beloved soulmate. Dr. El, this wondrous, beautiful man, who loved Avatar Meher Baba so very much and lived his talk of love—I thank you, El, for bringing me to Meher in this life. I thank you for the love you were and are. You will always be to me, so beautiful in my heart.

*****

El passed in 2003. Alexander and I were married in 2008. Today, we share the love of Baba, we share life. We have beautiful paintings of Baba in our home in Hendersonville, North Carolina, share His readings each and every day, and so enjoy visiting the Center. On the wall in our dining room, is a framed picture of Dr. El, whom we both will love and honor eternally. El was Baba's gift to both me and to Alexander. When I think of El, I think of a verse in Philippians 1:3, "I thank my God in all my remembrance of you." Meher Baba holds my heart. I feel Him in the simplest of things like the tree, the moment, beauty, loss, my joy, my tears, the face of a child. Baba is everything, the Ocean of love and He is found in every drop of His Ocean. Without me always being aware of it, Baba has directed each and every experience of my life. My gratitude for this gift to me is beyond words, as is my love for Him.

101 Tales of Finding Love

MY FORTY-FIVE-YEAR ROMANCE WITH MEHER BABA

by Max Reif

Meher Baba, the Ancient One 1925

Max Reif in Chicago 2006

I first encountered the name Meher Baba while walking to breakfast with an acquaintance at New College in Sarasota, Florida in early February 1969. My friend was carrying a newspaper, probably the New York Times, reading at it as we walked together silently. Half way to the cafeteria, he announced, "Here's an interesting article!" and proceeded to read a brief story on the obituary page. The piece went something like:

> *"There was a man named Meher Baba, who lived in India and did not speak. He maintained for many years that he was God, and would break his silence before he died. He died yesterday, January 31, 1969."*

My emotional response to those words was a kind of whimsical delight. That someone, somewhere in the modern world would either claim he was God, or maintain silence—let alone both—briefly lifted the quotidian veil, somehow. Before long, however, the name Meher Baba faded from my consciousness.

The context for that 'first hearing' described above, of course, was the cyclonic 1960s and its blast furnace of intensity, a vortex of energy replete with new possibilities and some peril, which actually lasted for me into the early eighties.

In the late sixties, many of us were too young or immature to know the stakes. I was feeling more and more lost, and like many, ended up playing Russian roulette with chemicals to try to find myself. I paid a heavy price, although I still believe it possible that God used drugs to batter down my ego, whose defenses were particularly self-protective because of traumatic experiences in childhood.

Hearing Meher Baba's name coincided with my plunge into the psychedelic world, followed by seven more plunges during the next year to try to recoup losses from the first time, as well as grab a golden key that always seemed to just elude me. Each effort to recover it failed, although it sometimes appeared briefly that I was on the way to success. After awhile, each experience just seemed to eat up part of me, so that by the end there was very little left.

The period also coincided with 'coming of age,' my twenty-first birthday, and with my expulsion from New College. Both events took place within two weeks of that memorable walk to breakfast. My mother keened on the phone when I told her of my expulsion, like an Irish woman who'd lost her fisherman son at sea.

I didn't feel consciously devastated, however. I felt I was moving toward something. A fellow New College student had offered the use of her family's land and farmhouse in upstate New York for an experimental community—a commune, as we called them. I felt this was my logical next step. Finally, away from meddling parents and university officials, I believed I could 'create—twenty-four hours a day.'

I left New College in a drive-away car with several friends, on what was their—but no longer my—spring break. It was my first cross-country drive, and my first time in California. It was all deliciously planned, this Grand Tour, to circle back for a quick visit with my folks, followed by the move to the farm.

By far the most poignant irony I'd ever experienced at that point in my life was a growing awareness, as I neared our utopia-to-be waiting outside of Ithaca: the closer I got, the more my mind was refusing to cooperate. I was falling into deep depression. Psychedelics had brought up deeply buried emotions I'd been defending against since childhood, and I was raw. My mind, it seems, was doing for me what I could not or would not do for myself, removing me from this unbearable nakedness by shutting me down completely.

Instead of realizing utopian dreams in the six months I spent at the farm, I became a living dead man. I tried to isolate from the other residents by putting a mattress down in the old milk room of the barn and making it 'my room,' leaving the farmhouse where everyone else lived. Finally, my parents came and begged me to come home. I vehemently refused. But one day not long after they left, I realized how deeply I was mired and that nothing would ever change if I stayed. I admitted defeat, caught a Greyhound, and became, for a year, my mother and father's child again.

The condition of living in the family home was that I see a psychiatrist once a week. I believed my case was hopeless, that the drugs had done something to my brain that was beyond repair. However, there was nothing to lose by complying with the request, and in fact it bought a year frozen in time that I look back on with great tenderness. After a couple of months of unsuccessful talking therapy, Dr. Wolff, the tall, gaunt psychiatrist, told me, "You are not responsible for your problems. You have a chemical imbalance. We will treat you with antidepressant pills, and we will keep trying different ones until one works."

Everyone today is conversant with 'chemical imbalances' and various brand names of antidepressants, but I had never heard of any of these things. Secretly, I didn't even really believe the doctor. How could my chemical imbalance just happen to coincide with the horrendous things I'd experienced on LSD? But again, I went along because there was nothing to lose. The period of trying different pills bought still more months of semi-pleasant limbo.

One day one of the pills worked. It was quite sudden. Instead of being afraid to leave the house without my parents, unable to think of anything to say to anyone, I was filled with energy and confidence. I marched into Dr. Wolff's office and proclaimed, "Out of the ashes we rise triumphant!"

I actually felt flooded by all the energy pumping into my system from whatever the pills had done. The doctor tried to explain it once—something about the pills "inhibiting the inhibitors" in my brain. It soon seemed I had exhausted the possibilities of my home city, even though it was holiday season and many friends were home from college. I decided to go visit old friends from my first college, Northwestern University in Evanston, Illinois. Having been very lonely most of my first year away from home there, I'd undergone a kind of awakening in the spring and had become a political radical. However, the end of a love affair during sophomore year had wounded me so much that I had transferred to New College rather than to go back as a junior.

With my new energy, which seemed to keep streaming no matter what happened, I enjoyed the three-hundred-mile drive from St. Louis. On the street near campus, I ran into a girl I'd known. She invited me to stay in the apartment she shared with a friend, and also mentioned, "Ellis is back in town!" Ellis Pines was the radical leader at whose Student Power election rally I had climbed onto a large boulder on campus and told my story of being roughed up by campus security.

He had been elected student president and a few months later had received a letter from the university, saying "You are disqualified from taking office because of a summer school course you didn't complete two years ago."

Disillusioned, he had left Evanston. Six weeks later my roommate and I, with whom he had stayed before leaving, had received a postcard from him written on a beach in Mexico, saying only, "Truth is metaphysical, not political."

The next thing I'd heard about Ellis was that he had somehow become connected with Meher Baba, the spiritual figure whose name I'd heard several more times since that day at New College, and one of whose books I had even perused, to little avail. After informing me of Ellis' return, my female friend added, "But you don't want to have anything to do with him. He works in an advertising agency now, and I saw him on TV selling laundry detergent!"

That telegraphic description, coupled with the image I'd had of him from before, created a picture that did indeed encourage me to give my old friend a wide berth. How had he possibly changed so much in two years?

In the next two weeks, I visited all my friends in Evanston except for Ellis. Practically every place I went, my host or hostess would point out in the bookcase a Meher Baba book he had brought by. Then, instead of discussing Meher Baba, we would continue to go on about Ellis and his recent eccentricity.

One morning, shortly before I intended to leave Chicago, the ringing telephone wakened me from a strange dream. The dream had uncannily been more vivid than waking life, something I had not even been aware could happen. It seemed to tell in symbols a version of my life story that frightened me, with 'the Tribe,' the organization of athletic lettermen at my high school, marching into the locker room where I was sitting and beating me into un-consciousness.

I did not have long to consider the dream right then, because one of my female hosts was nudging me and saying, "You have a phone call!"

The receiver to my ear, I heard a voice say, "Hi, this is Ellis! I heard you were in town, and that you're doing well, and I was so happy to hear that!" I immediately felt disarmed by his genuine, friendly tone. There was no eccentricity about it, only simple humanity. He went on to invite me to stop by the advertising agency where he worked to say hello before leaving town. I did not feel in the least bit anxious, replying that I'd love to.

The next morning I took the El train downtown to the Pruden-tial Building, where my friend worked. I caught the elevator to his ad agency on the upper floors. Notified by the receptionist, Ellis came out to the front area and embraced me. Then he led me down a corridor and opened a doorway into what was the tiniest private office I'd ever seen.

There were a desk and two chairs in the office—no room for anything else. One of the chairs was behind the desk, the other in front. I sat, of course, in the latter. As I faced my friend, I noticed that behind him on the wall was a large poster on yellow newsprint paper. A man's face, in a black and white photo, looked out from the poster. The man appeared to be in his twenties. He had long straight hair, a feathery moustache, a wisp of beard, and the loveliest soft, clear eyes. Under the photo in large letters were the words:

I AM

THE ANCIENT ONE

I was Rama, I was Krishna,

I was this one, I was that one,

And now I am Meher Baba.

Suddenly I realized that sitting in front of me was someone who could tell me more about this unusual man whose obituary had been read to me for some unknown reason on a misty Saturday morning two years before.

"Did Meher Baba really say he was God?" I asked.

"He says everyone and everything is God, but there are very few who are fully conscious of that Divinity and who therefore are really able to guide others."

"Why shouldn't I follow Christ or Ramakrishna?" The question erupted out of my mouth. It included the names of two spiritual beings I had recently begun reading about—Sri Ramakrishna having been a great Master who had lived near Calcutta in the late nineteenth century.

"Baba said he's the Avatar," Ellis replied. "He said he returns to Earth approximately every seven to fourteen hundred years, whenever people forget why we're really here. In recorded history, he said he had previously come as Zoroaster, Rama, Krishna, Buddha, Jesus and Mohammed."

"He's naming the greatest figures in history," I thought. I was experiencing a curious phenomenon. Questions had been coming to my mind as naturally as though I were following some kind of script. And yet my words were totally spontaneous. Furthermore, each time my friend answered a question, or more accurately, told me Meher Baba's answer, I felt lighter. White birds seemed to be flying upward from my head, so to speak, and taking shadows with them, with every round of our conversation.

After a few more questions and answers, the process stopped. My mind and the room were silent. "Maybe this Meher Baba was a really great man," the voice of my thoughts went on, "but if he died two years ago, what's the difference?" As that thought emerged, a very subtle presentiment, came with it—something might happen now. That was odd. My sense that "nothing can happen through mere conversation" had led, a couple of years back, to my more dangerous, pharmacologically based efforts at transformation.

"Where is he now?" I blurted out, looking at Meher Baba's picture and not even realizing I'd been about to speak.

I waited for Ellis to answer. Silence. In a little while, I looked back toward him. He was smiling. What about? He in fact wore practically the widest grin I'd ever seen. I had seen him grinning that way once back in our college days, scruffily dressed, high on LSD and gleefully handing a five dollar bill to a beggar.

And then, suddenly, I felt it, too, the—Love! This was Love! Not Romantic Love, not platonic love with a small 'p', but Divine Love! I'd read of it recently in Thomas Merton and in Christopher Isherwood's *Ramakrishna and His Disciples*, but without much idea what the authors were talking about. This was God!

The room overflowed with Divine Love! The force, the Being, was invisible, yet far more real by far than anything I'd ever known. It felt 'pink' somehow, although visually I discerned no color. "I am Meher Baba," it seemed to be saying, silently, a distinct Personality that also somehow included Ellis and me, and everything else! Words like 'past' and 'future,' 'me' and 'you' had no meaning. Only this timeless, all-embracing Love had ever existed.

How had I never before felt what was clearly the only essential fact of all existence? How had I failed to notice Meher Baba, who was and had always been, the Being of my own being, the Self of all?

How long Ellis and I sat there, embraced by that divine Smile, I don't know. But when I left that room, as it says in a poem I penned a few years later, "I searched a different search and sang a different tune."

Postscript:

I left that room forty-five years ago. Not too long after, I quit taking the antidepressant pills because although they supplied energy, I no longer felt they really balanced me the way my doctor had said. I no longer believe pills can accomplish that herculean labor, although I can't judge anyone's use of whatever seems to help, even temporarily, in this difficult life.

I had a girl friend by then, and came to feel that in some subtle way, the pills made it impossible for me to bring my true, vulnerable self to our relationship. I took myself off them, thinking "Baba will take care of me now." But I had karma to reckon with, and spent another year and a half in a black hole.

I don't want to romanticize my life since my initial profound experience of Meher Baba. Such an experience, resulting in conviction about the Master's status, is colloquially known as "coming to Baba." Adi K. Irani, Baba's longtime secretary, spoke of it as "God-realization in disguise."

However, living the life of literal obedience that Baba asks of those who love Him has been compared by His close disciple Eruch Jessawala, to walking on fire all the time. I don't feel I've been completely successful at that, this lifetime. I would describe myself as a spiritual amphibian climbing out of the seas of ignorance. I've had precipitous falls and periods of suffering after coming to Baba. What is noteworthy, I feel, is to have been able to recover and go on. Baba said, "All suffering is your labor of love to unveil your real Self. And someday," He also said, "the labor will be complete!"

*****

I currently live in Walnut Creek, California with my wife, Barbara. I work thirty hours a week as a preschool aftercare teacher at Meher School in nearby Lafayette; volunteer for White Pony Express, a Baba-related food rescue program; and try use the rest of my time to further my remembrance of the Beloved, and hopefully to occasionally clear the way for something creative to emerge.

101 Tales
of Finding Love

A TIMELESS MOMENT

by Irma Sheppard

Meher Baba 1927

Irma with Christine and Scott Meherabad 1981

Ifirst saw a picture of Meher Baba in July, 1975—a card fastened above the rearview mirror of Donald Hill's VW camper—Meher Baba standing, looking like Jesus. It made no impression on me, except that I never forgot that I saw it.

I met Donald on a park bench in Piraeus, Greece. I happened to be there through a series of unusual events.

I had been teaching English As a Second Language in Ferndale, a town just north of Detroit. A young Greek couple came into my Beginning ESL class—George already had some English and moved on quickly, but Mary stayed in my class till their son, Zach, was born. We became friends. After two years they prepared to return to his family travel agency in Athens, Greece. "Come visit us," they said. I'd have loved to, but I was a single mom—no time or money for such a trip.

A few months later I received an unexpected, substantial tax refund. Then my (former) in-laws, who had recently retired to Florida, asked if they could have my daughter, nine, and son, six, for one month in the summer. "Yes," I said. Then my former husband asked if our children could stay with him and his new wife for a month in the summer. I said yes. So all of a sudden I had time and money to visit George and Mary in Athens! I told everyone, "I'm going to Athens! I'm going to Greece!"

I spent a couple of days with George, Mary and Zach in Athens. George had made flight arrangements for Mary, Zach and me to fly to Samos, an island near Turkey, where her mother lived. It was the custom for women and children to leave Athens each summer to get the fresh air of the Greek islands. While Mary was pregnant and unhappy about this plan, I was just so excited to be out in the world again that I didn't mind at all.

Saturday morning we arrived at the domestic airport early and got in line. When we reached the desk, there was a flurry of discussion, protest and indignation in Greek, then George turned to me in despair and said I'd been bumped off the flight. I had to stay in Athens with George until Monday, when he'd booked me on a flight to Samos.

Again, I didn't mind and spent the morning shopping and exploring downtown Athens. It occurred to me that I could take the subway to Piraeus, the seaport where the movie, "Never on Sunday" had been filmed with Melina Mercouri as a good-hearted prostitute. My best friend, Marti, and I had greatly enjoyed listening to that song in English, in German, in Italian and in Greek. We danced to it at the Caboto Club in Windsor, Canada, {where I grew up} and generally made a minor fetish of Melina and the song. So I had to see Piraeus.

Once there, I wandered through the open market stalls, which displayed mainly carpentry tools and butchered pig haunches with complementary flies. I wondered what I had expected, why I had come, and felt oddly embarrassed, foolish and disappointed. By late afternoon I was tired, and headed for a nearby park looking for a bench—but what I saw were clusters of men near the entrance. Hmm. With Melina's occupation in the film in mind, I realized I didn't know what the customs were in this place. I exited and circled the park till I found an area with women and children. On a bench there I wrote in my new Greek notebook—my first journal since high school. Then I opened a magazine.

"Is that the latest *Time* magazine?" The grey-haired man who had sat down on the other end of the bench was not Greek as I'd thought. This was Donald, the black sheep of a Boston banking family. He had just seen friends off by ship to Crete. I told him my story about Samos. I have no memory of how we got onto the subject of extraordinary experiences, but within half an hour of chatting, I told him something I'd never told anyone—something I'd experienced when I was fifteen.

In 1958 at fourteen, I started attending Lutheran confirmation classes with our pastor every Friday after school. My parents were not religious, but followed the conventions of their own upbringing as far as religion went. Somehow I came to believe that when I'd had my first communion, I would be altered, my life would be altered. This conviction was very important to me, as there was a great deal of dysfunction and abuse in my family. I was desperate for change.

On Palm Sunday the confirmation class sat in the front pew. In response to the questions put to us, we stood and recited creeds, psalms, lists of Old and New Testament books, and so on. Then at the rail before the altar we received communion. As I walked back to my seat, the pasty wafer stuck to the roof of my mouth and the thimbleful of sweet wine tickled my throat. That was all. As I wrote in a poem decades later, I experienced "not a trace of even the smallest grace." Disappointment was profound. And I had no one to tell.

In September of that year, my older sister and I took a train from Windsor, Canada to Long Island, New York to attend a cousin's wedding. An aunt lent us a book, *The Search for Bridey Murphy,* about reincarnation. Reading this electrified me—I knew this was true—reincarnation was a fact. Having this book in hand was so important to me that I took it home to Windsor without daring to ask my aunt for it. In October I turned fifteen.

Then in November as I was trying to go to sleep one night, I suddenly found myself in an altered state of consciousness. In this state I had no awareness of my body, only a sense of widening rising spirals. I *knew* that I was not this body, this identity of 'Irma.' I was something else, something far beyond that. I don't know how long I was in that state, but when I came out of it, all I wanted was to go back. But I didn't know how. In the morning I had only the question "Who am I?" With no one to talk to.

This is what I told Donald on the park bench.

It took over forty years before I connected those two events of 1958—the fervent desire/need for real change and the altered state of consciousness. Recently I read in *Lord Meher* that on one night in November 1958, Baba said He'd spent the whole night remembering His lovers all over the world...making an offering of His love to them. I tell myself that He thought of me that night, perhaps laid or activated a cable between us.

Back in Piraeus, Donald seemed to know what I was talking about regarding this experience of an altered state. I was impressed since I'd never told anyone before. We had dinner together that evening, then I returned to George's apartment. His sister was there to chaperone us. I met Donald the next day and we went to the beach in his camper. I must have seen Baba's picture then.

I was eighteen the last time I had gone to my church. I realized I would not find answers to my questions there. At university I took philosophy and psychology, thinking they'd have the answers I was looking for. They did not. The experience I'd had at fifteen had apparently opened my awareness to something beyond academia. Eventually I gave up all creeds, keeping God, Jesus and the Golden Rule. That did not keep me from making lots of mistakes and only slowly, gradually learning from them. Questions cycled in my head: *What does all this mean? What is the purpose?*

Shortly before my first husband and I divorced, I had an intense dream. Walking in the city I heard the high-pitched whinnying of a horse in terror. I came upon the horse, tethered so tightly to a garage that it could not stand—it was rearing and screaming incessantly. The horse was white. It signified to me how I felt being tightly constrained in this marriage.

Donald's story was that he was on his way to India. He, his wife Kathy and their four-year-old daughter Pagan, had set out from Amsterdam, traveled through France and Spain to Marrakech, where they had a falling out and separated. He was now still headed for India on his own. As we met, he was set to sail to

Crete to join his friends on Monday, just as I was to fly to Samos. We agreed to stay in touch via the American Express office bulletin board, and reunite in Athens in a few weeks. We did just that.

We spent half of July and all of August camping around the Peleponnesian peninsula, visiting also the Delphic Oracle. It was heaven. I missed my children and wished fervently that they could have enjoyed this adventure with me. But this turned out to be my 'honeymoon' with Donald, complete with hash pipe and attendant physical pleasures. We shared our respective histories and adventures, played Scrabble every day at some beach café. I said to him once, "I can love you, Donald." He responded in kind. We were high on hash, but it felt true to me. I asked him once, "Who is that in picture over the rearview mirror?"

"An Indian holy man," he said. Or something like that. I didn't pursue it.

Donald asked me to go with him to India. (He and Kathy had attended the 1969 Darshan, but he didn't tell me that while we were in Greece.) I'd never had such an exotic invitation. "I can't," I said. "I have two children, a job, a house—I can't just disappear on them." At the end of August he took me to the airport where, due to the massive crowd, we didn't have a proper leave-taking. I felt panicky as I boarded the plane. *I couldn't lose touch with this man!*

As soon as I arrived home in Ferndale, Michigan, I wrote to Donald in care of American Express: "Dear Donald, I want to see you again. Do you want to see me?" A few weeks later I received his reply: "Yes."

In the year and a half it took him to show up at my home, I'd reverted to my previous lifestyle of letting men cycle in and out of my life. In hindsight I saw this as my desperate attempts to fill an emptiness that felt hopeless. When Donald finally came, I cleared away the last of these men, thinking I now had someone I could make a life with. Within six months, I sold my home, sold or gave away everything in it, sadly agreed with my son that he could go live with his father, traded my hatchback Gremlin for a 1974 VW poptop camper and quit my job. On June 6, 1977 Donald, Stephanie, eleven, and I drove off on a five-month camping trip across the United States, ending up in Venice Beach, California. This journey was a true adventure, but it was not heaven. I began to see some of Donald's shortcomings, as well as my own.

Donald introduced me to Sufi thought, Buddhism, Ram Dass and others. From time to time he'd say something about "Meher Baber" in his Boston accent. He never said much about him, but one time in Venice Beach Donald quoted something Baba had said. I don't remember what it was, but I said, "Who does he think he is, God?"

"He says He is," Donald said. I didn't say anything, but thought, *this one says he's God, that one says he's God, you're God, I'm God, we're all God.*

I woke up one morning in Venice Beach with a compelling voice ringing in my head. *You will know everything you need to know when you need to know it.* There was no image—just this message. It was strangely comforting.

After a lifetime of suffering from asthma, smoking non-filtered Camels and dope (hashish, marijuana), Donald, who was twenty years older than I, suffered from emphysema. By this time, Stephanie and I had sadly agreed that she would be better off living with her father and brother in Illinois. Donald's daughter, Pagan, had come to live with us at age seven, and was now nine. His grown son, Richard, also lived with us for a couple of years. Four of us in two rooms, half a block from the Pacific. With his year-long illness, our relationship had changed—I was now part caregiver of Donald and part caretaker of Pagan. I felt the walls of illusion had become more slippery than ever—I needed something to hang on to.

Before he was too ill to drive, Donald went to some meetings at the Meher Baba Center of Southern California on Santa Monica Boulevard. He brought home a large poster of Baba with the message, "Don't Worry, Be Happy," and put it up in the galley kitchen. Something in Baba's eyes held me.

One day after closing the activities room at the Santa Monica board and care home where I was the recreation director, I spread a mat on the floor. I sat and began to chant, *om nam renge kyo*. After just a few minutes I stopped—my heart wasn't into it. Silence. In desperation, I said, *Whoever, Whatever there Is, please help me.*

On the first day of spring 1980, Donald died. Kathy and Richard came from the east coast to deal with Donald's cremation and to sort through his belongings. We all got on well. I felt an aura of love as we each did our tasks and I assumed it was Donald's love for us—all working together now. Only later did it occur to me that I was experiencing Meher Baba's love. At one point I heard Kathy say, "If anyone wants these things about Meher Baba, please take them. Otherwise I will. I just don't want them to be thrown away." My ears shot to attention. *Meher Baba! She knows about Meher Baba!* I went to look at what she had: the poster, the card from their VW camper in Greece and a book, *Listen, Humanity.*

"I'll take them," I said.

A week later Kathy, Pagan and Richard were gone and I was alone in grief, loss and exhaustion. I returned to my job at the board and care home, but after a few weeks I was wrongfully fired. It was a blessing for me—my own health was suffering from stress and smoking, and I couldn't really do the job anymore. I received unemployment benefits. Doing yoga early one morning I injured my neck. Days later, I lay in bed with a cervical collar around my neck, in pain with any movement, looking at the poster, "Don't Worry, Be Happy." I thought, *I don't know how to do that.* The kindness in His eyes was all I had to hang on to.

I read *Listen, Humanity.* It answered all the questions I ever had, and it answered questions I didn't even know I had. As I read I was aware of wanting to believe that Meher Baba was who He said He was.

I remembered that some months earlier, Donald, Pagan and I had seen three films of the Dalai Lama. I watched his devotees approach him, each one putting a white shawl around his neck, and he putting his hand on each of their heads in blessing as they bowed before him with folded hands. And a longing had come through me—I wanted someone to go to, to trust, to guide me. Desperately wanted.

There came a moment, perhaps in May or early June, a timeless moment—of such depth that ever since, when I speak of it, tears come—when I experienced the conviction, the *knowing,* that Meher Baba was Who He said He was. And so turned my face to Love as I had never known. *He is Who He says He is—God in human form.* My next thought was, "Irma, you're getting weird. You've been alone too long." But the conviction never went away.

Years later, in 2003, when I told Don Stevens about this, he said, "So, you have experienced the Presence of the Master." I had never thought of it that way—that there in the solitude my little studio apartment, in sight of the Pacific Ocean, Baba had given me His darshan.

For days I felt an unparalleled joy. God had been here on earth. Just twelve years ago!

While I had always believed in Jesus, I never felt close to Him. He seemed so far, far away. I remembered when I was thirteen, at a time that was particularly dark in my family, and I urgently needed help—real help. I knelt at my bedside at night and said The Lord's Prayer over and over, *trying so hard to mean every word,* wanting Jesus, God to hear me. A few days later I did receive a solution (though I didn't recognize it as that till many years later), and this kept me safe from that particular danger in my family.

One night in Venice Beach I dreamt of an otter floating on its back in the ocean, rinsing clams in the water and eating them. When I woke, I knew I was that otter, sustained by the Ocean—nourished, supported, at ease.

I went to my first Baba meeting on Friday, June 13, 1980—my lucky day. I had barely settled into a rear seat when Adele Wolkin made her way to a seat two rows in front of me. She sat, turned to look at me with her big blue eyes and asked a question about the program—as if I would know. She looked at me as if she'd known me all my life. Yes, I was in the right place!

After that, despite pain and grief, I went to every meeting, listened hungrily to all the stories of those who had lived with or met Baba. I realized later how fortunate I was that so many told their stories of being with Baba. Filis Frederick, Adele Wolkin, Jean Adriel, Bili Eaton, Alan Cohen, Robert Dreyfuss, Ursula Reinhart, and many more. When I heard there was to be a sahavas with a *dhuni*, I knew I had to go—it was the only way I could stop smoking. I went to the July 4th Sahavas at Pilgrim Pines, wept copiously as I heard the heartful stories of Don Stevens, Charles Haynes and others, and heard the songs of love to the Beloved and saw, for the first time, His graceful form moving about in the film "O Parvardigar."

I watched people kneel at and bow down to plaster casts of Baba's feet, set before the dhuni. I had never knelt or bowed down to anyone in my life. Would I kneel, bow down? I pondered whether to throw in all smoking or just cigarettes. Perhaps I didn't make up my mind until, *yes*! I knelt there myself and with a stick of sandalwood dipped in ghee, threw all smoking into the dhuni. It took that attachment clean away!

A feeling that I had to leave Los Angeles grew within me, that my life was not there, but I had no idea where to go or what to do with myself. In October I sold my VW camper. At the Baba meetings I kept hearing talk about *Amartithi* in Meherabad, India. *Oh, that's where I'll go!*

Irma Sheppard

Five years earlier in Greece, Donald had asked me to go to India with him, and I'd said no because I had two children, a house, a job. Now they were all gone, Donald too. Baba had removed them, one by one, and I was free, on my own, to go to Him.

On my third trip to India in October, 1996, as I stood in the parking lot across the road from the International Airport in Mumbai, I heard Baba's voice:

So now you are coming to Me?
Yes.
And you will be Mine?
Yes.
Forever.
Yes.
And I will take care of you.
Yes.
Don't worry. I will take care of everything.
Yes.

*****

Now I live with my husband, Karl, and our dear cat, Sasha, in Asheville, North Carolina. In 2016 we moved here from Tucson, Arizona. I feel fortunate to live among a large, active community of Baba lovers here. I have retired from psychotherapy work and still write occasional poems. Meher Baba kindly gave me this project of collecting stories of how His lovers came to know His Love. How He drew us to Himself with His love, using both our strengths and weaknesses to best advantage.

101 Tales of Finding Love

'THE FIRST TIME EVER I SAW....'

by Wayne Smith

Wayne with Eruch Jessawala 1988

Wayne with Don Stevens 2006

....When I call out your name, When I say your name, When I speak your name, When I whisper Your name, When I write your name, When I imagine your name, When I think your name, When I sing your name, When I pray your name, When I see your name, When I ask your name, When I use your name, When I shout your name.... Your name.... Your name...Meher Baba...Your name is all there is for me now...Baba, Baba, Baba...Are you not always there...do You ever not reply....

Towards the end of 1985 I found myself living in Lancaster, in the north of England, studying Eastern Religions and Philosophy at the University there. Nineteen, turning twenty, I was seeking answers to the big questions of life, but was still quite lost and very much unfound. In short, in limbo-land—that half-way house between the dissolute waywardness of a past that I could so easily slide back into, and the desperate need for something more spiritually substantial and sustaining. But what—I knew not, nor how or why or where?

I had already been interested in mysticism for some time, and Buddhism in particular since the age of sixteen. At University I took this one step further by attending a weekly *zazen* meditation group affiliated with the Soto Zen retreat based at Throssel Hall in Northumberland. Even so, I thirsted for more—that 'divine desperation' Baba refers to had well and truly taken me in its grip. I just knew with all of my being that something more was needed—personal guidance and connection with the Universal Reality which at the time I could only term 'Buddha Nature.'

And then the 'Master' appeared—in the form of a face—a captivating Christ-like face. It was one which transfixed me from the posters which had appeared, as if by magic, to grace virtually every pillar in the main square of the campus. On closer inspection I saw that it advertised a film and music event celebrating the life of somebody called Meher Baba to be held at the University Chaplaincy Centre. Instantly impelled I took one and, pleased as Baba punch, I stole my treasure back to the caravan I lived in at the time. It was perched high on the moors looking west over Morecambe Bay and the mountains of Lake Land, a great place for sunsets and star-gazing. There I did the only thing I knew how to do—stuck the poster on the wall a foot above the ground and began to mediate on it. Over the course of the next few weeks I became completely lost in the eyes and captivated by the face of this personage known as Meher Baba. By the day of the actual event, some weeks later, I could think of little else.

Eventually the evening arrived in the early Spring of 1986. I vaguely remember many speakers and some music, but it was the film I saw, "Meher Baba's Call," that made the biggest, most last-ing impression on me. For it only confirmed even more so in my heart that here was the one—that He was the One—the personal guide my soul had been seeking for so long. There were two occa-sions in the film when I had the distinct experience that the fig-ure on the screen was somebody divine.

The first occurred where Baba, on top of a car, is being driven slowly through the amassed crowds. He puts his hands together and turns towards the camera. In that moment I just knew this man was God and in some way, that he was One with all that he saw around him and that saw him. The other occasion is when a nurse washes a leper with the utmost humility and care. The two are standing up and she is dressed in white, wearing a headscarf. My experience is that this act is so completely selfless that there are not two bodies here, but one—again, just an experience of complete Oneness. It is as if the nurse is washing herself, is not aware of any difference between where her body ends and the other's begins—whatsoever. In time I would learn that this 'nurse' was in fact Baba himself.

The following months I nearly flunked my degree, for all I wanted to know about and immerse myself in was Meher Baba. By this time, having been snowed in one too many times, I had moved from the isolation of my caravan into the town itself. The walls of the converted garage I 'sublet' from some friends became bedecked in countless images of Baba. I would spend a day a week in silence, fasting, beginning to learn how to pray again and even to familiarise myself with the word 'God.' One of the courses I was studying (entitled 'New Modern Religious Movements') even featured Meher Baba himself. Moreover, the lecturer had obtained for the University library every known book on His life and teachings. I set about reading them all. Furthermore, I also met (through my friend Rob who also attended the zazen group) the two local Baba lovers who had organised the event—Avril and Netta—and started to attend their group meetings. The beginning of my coming to Baba had begun.

One distinct aspect of that initial 'honeymoon' phase which further convinced me of Baba's divinity and Avatarhood, were the recollection of two dreams that I'd had in childhood. The first had always remained with me, in fact had become one of the most vivid and vital experiences of my early years. In it I find myself looking down from above, over the most beautiful arcadian landscape, full of light and warmth and colour. I focus in upon an enchanting woodland at the heart of which lies a forest glade. The deciduous trees are quite openly spaced and the sunlight comes streaming through—it feels like heaven. And then through the shimmering leaves I see a horse, the most beautiful pure white horse that I have ever seen, stepping its way very slowly and consciously towards the glade. It is the most incredible creature, entirely enrapturing, and on its back a rider with long black hair. They enter the glade and then, seeming to become aware of me, they both look in my direction. In that moment I am filled with the most indescribable feeling of happiness, the like of which I have never experienced before. I am completely overcome with joy, in absolute bliss.

Looking back, I seemed to encounter white horses in various significant ways throughout my childhood—from popular songs of the day to the kitsch print that greeted me in the hallway of my grandparents' house whenever I would visit. I can still see myself as that small child gazing up, completely enchanted and absorbed within its landscape—those beautiful, snowy white horses dancing in the surf on the beach of some dream-like world. Still to this day I am transported by white horses, glimpsed occasionally, for example, through the window of some passing car or train, standing tall in a field, or against the skyline on some ancient Welsh mountain-side.

At the other extreme, the second dream could best be described as a nightmare. It was a repetitive one, full of such absolute terror and fear as to invariably result in my fighting to free myself awake from its terrifying grip—arms flailing, soaking in sweat, suffocating and full of tears. Desperate for the comforting embrace of my mother, who would often hear my waking cry, I was always too terrified to fall back asleep, back to that place where—I seem to be aware only of space—deep, black, infinite space. It is all around me—everywhere. There is a humming and then a hand, bigger than anything I have ever seen before, towering above me—its size is beyond belief—as large as a child's universe. The thumb and adjacent finger of this hand press together and between them is me! Or as I imagine it at that age, my head, my self, my very being—tinier than the tiniest pea—being pressed down and squashed away. And there seems to be no escape. The massiveness of the hand, the minisculeness of 'me' being pressed out of existence, excruciatingly slowly and irrevocably. Being squashed away, into nothingness. I can only stand so much of this process before I have to claw my way back to the surface, out of the nightmare, as if I'd been drowning, fighting for air, for my very existence, out of this sleep, soaking and tearful.

This nightmare occurred several times over a number of years and then was no more—not even a memory, but something so traumatic as to necessarily become completely suppressed somewhere deep inside. That is until the day when, shortly after I had first heard about Meher Baba, I was looking through the book, *The Beloved*, when I encountered it again—that hand, its finger and thumb pressed together to form a circle. Except that this time it was attached to Baba Himself as He sat in an armchair, smiling knowingly at the camera. In a flash it all came back, though this time without the feeling of terror, and I became even more certain that Meher Baba was who He said He was—the Avatar, God in human form—my 'Master,' the only one for me. Yes, He was the Awakener—in the truest and most absolute sense—even if His idea of awakening sometimes has to occur though the medium of nightmares!

Dreams continued to play an important part in my relationship with Baba, and some were more real and moving than anything else that I have experienced in my waking life, though they seem to occur less and less so as time flows by. In retrospect I think that they have tended to occur when I have been in particular need of Baba's helping hand, even if I was slow to realise or take it fully at the time. There have been perhaps five or six which I count as being so vital as to actually provide me with an experience of Baba's presence—His love, His glance and, on occasion, His enfolding arms so full of such overwhelming, enveloping love that I would invariably dissolve into an uncontrollable waterfall of tears.

Almost three years after I first encountered Baba's face on that poster I found myself on my first ever plane flight heading for India. It was the autumn of 1988 and I was travelling with Rob—the only other person to have come to Baba following the event. As you can imagine a trip to India at this time for two twenty-three-year-olds had all of the challenges you can imagine. We arrived at a Mumbai airport the worse for wear and immediately found ourselves overwhelmed on all five sensory fronts before we had even left the relatively safe confines of the airport. The heat was completely new to me, the intensity of the light, the bright, primary colours, the exotic smells.

But what proved most challenging were the people: that great variety and press of humanity that seemed to assail us from all sides as soon as we had left the airport gates; the countless hands trying to help us with our luggage; the countless voices trying to vie for our attention and trade. We had no plan except that we knew we had to travel to a city called 'Poona,' followed by a town called Ahmednagar and then arrive at our true 'home'—*Meherabad*—that long-awaited paradise. This was before the days of websites and guidance from the Trust office. We had a small booklet entitled, if I remember rightly, *Welcome Home*, but nothing else except an address at King's Road, Ahmednagar. Completely at a loss we decided to fly to Pune—how we had arrived at this decision I cannot now recollect—but fly we did from the Domestic airport.

We scrambled into a taxi and made our way there. The heat, the lack of air conditioning meant that we desperately needed the windows open, but then the dilemma of how to avoid the constant hands trying to push through, and the faces and gestures imploring charity from us. We had little choice but to suffer the heat as the car pressed its way slowly though the dense crowd. From here on in, until we reached our destination, there are blurred edges to my recollections—largely the product, I should think, of a great deal of uncertainty combined with a good dose of fear of the unknown.

All I now remember is flying over the Western Ghats during what I came to later realise was a potentially fatal combination of darkness and torrential monsoon rains and lightening. People around me seemed to be using rosary beads and praying out loud. For myself, on only my second ever flight, I just assumed that all was normal and to be expected. By the time we reached Pune all the electricity was out in the city and the plane had to attempt more than one landing before it could finally touch down safely on a runway lit by bonfires. In 1988 Pune airport seemed little more than a shack, and we had to walk across the runaway to exit the airport; by the time we had found a rickshaw we were completely soaked.

There seemed very little language spoken that seemed to be understood over the next few days, but people seemed to understand what we needed and were asking for. The rickshaw driver careered us through the night along 'roads' that resembled muddy streams, veering from one side to the other in a vain attempt to avoid vast puddles, oncoming traffic, animals and people in an increasingly manic journey that took us deeper and deeper into the unknown.

Eventually we found ourselves at an Indian guest-house. More gestures and broken English found us in a room the likes of which I had never imagined existing, let alone encountered before: bare furnishings, a barely functioning bathroom, cracked tiles, peeling wallpaper behind which cockroaches lurked and would emerge whenever the lights went out—a single bare light bulb which had to stay on all night to deter them. A second sleepless night awaited us.

At some stage our hunger drove us to brave the dining room downstairs. There seemed to be as a sea of incredulous faces no doubt astonished at these two Western boys attempting to eat from an Indian *thali* plate. No knives and forks, just a spoon and an assortment of small steel bowls positioned within a larger one. All the assembled staff and waiters looked at us waiting to see what would happen next. There was only one thing to do: we emptied all of the contents of the smaller into the larger in one fell swoop and spooned the swimming contents down as fast as we could before fleeing back to our room.

The next morning I cannot remember if breakfast was eaten or even offered—we were very conscious from our booklet of eating the wrong things and being struck by the dreaded 'Delhi belly' everybody had kindly warned us about. But I do know that the constant fear I had for our lives was due to get a whole lot worse. A car was produced to taxi us to Ahmednagar and we were both relieved to know that our ordeal would soon be over.

However, only a matter of minutes after setting off to our 'home' a short time after being bundled into it we found ourselves taken to some other area of Pune. The driver got out and went into a building. We were left alone. I was sure that this was it—the end had come—at the best what awaited us would be robbery and theft, especially when our 'driver' emerged with a group of other men. "Well, Baba," I remember thinking, "...so near, yet so far." One of the other men got in. No communication whatsoever with us, just exchanges with the others in some unknown tongue.

Then the ignition turned over and we set of again with our lives and possessions intact. Phew!

Sometime later—it seemed like several hours, but was maybe only a handful—we arrived in the outskirts of Ahmednagar. More uncertainty awaited us though when we realised that our driver had become lost and had to ask for directions. However, by this stage I was so tired and maybe becoming more acquainted with Baba's twists-and-turns that it seemed to matter less, for I knew that gradually, step by step, we were getting closer. I also remember thinking that surely everybody, just everybody must know of the whereabouts of this sacred place of the Avatar of the Age! I was wrong. The driver had to stop several folk before we found a group who actually seemed to know, but eventually the car pulled down a little side-street towards what literally seemed to be a dead end. Another false trail, I thought. We had stopped before some tall gates.

And then we noticed it—Baba's name. At last, we'd finally arrived! Then the gates opened and we walked inside—we had finally made it—we were home at last! The first thing that struck me was the stillness and the quiet, and then the complete absence of anybody else. It was all in sharp, complete contrast to the dust and the noise and the mayhem and vast multitudes of people that we had just been subject to. Here there was no one—just a simple paradise of quiet and light and trees and flowers and birdsong. We just stood there and grinned and held a hand out to each other.

After a time out of time a figure emerged from the right walking quickly across the compound. She looked up at us and smiled so beautifully. It was Mani—Meher Baba's beloved sister! She was as amazed to see us as we to see her. In those days visitors were less frequent of course, especially two not-quite-so-fresh-faced young men who just seemed to turn up out of nowhere. Dear Mani, she immediately took us under her wing and led us to the office for registration. Over the next two weeks her 'English boys' would be well looked after by her. Unfortunately we were too late to be taken to the Pilgrim Centre and found ourselves in another Indian hotel with, let's say, a different kind of experience to the one we'd had the night before.

The next day we were there. And then the walk up that hill, the one I had been envisaging, imagining for so long, to be welcomed home, literally, by Nana Kher and given prasad by Mansari. I had finally reached my Beloved's Samadhi—the very centre of the known universe. I was finally home!

...Such a love that has brought me here...Some days it's as if I simply awake to remember YOU....that only You ARE...that only You are REAL...Only You, and everything else an illusion, everything mere shadow play.... I'm so glad to be alive so that I can know You...I settle in this body, because of Your love, to stand at this moment and in this place, to think only of You, my Meher Baba, and to know that You alone are Real....

POSTSCRIPT:

The following day, a Tuesday, was a 'Meherazad day' and I knew exactly where I wanted to go when we had arrived: the place I considered second only to the Samadhi in the whole world—Baba's room. I cannot remember how I knew where it was, but as soon as the bus arrived I leapt off and made my way purposefully there. At that time pilgrims were far fewer than they are now and I managed to reach the room first with nobody else around. At least that's what I thought, for just as I was about to take off my sandals, I noticed the figure of a man with his back to me enjoying the plants and flowers that were planted nearby. He turned around and introduced himself—it was Don Stevens. The name was familiar, I had seen it on a few of the books I had read at University, but really knew nothing about the man. He kindly offered to show me around Baba's room and the two of us stepped inside. Dear Don was so courteous and considerate—it felt almost as if he was introducing me to Baba himself. After a few minutes he said he would leave so I could be alone with Baba.

After paying my respects in Baba's room I then made my way to the porch and was introduced, I'm almost sure, to the women mandali by Don himself. Overcome by the occasion and in full hugging mode I staggered towards Mehera, but was gently reminded that a hug was not possible. Oh, the *faux pas* of the greenhorn! And then to Mandali Hall to meet the man who I would come to consider my 'spiritual grandfather'—Eruch. I may even have managed a climb up Seclusion Hill, though maybe that had to wait until my return on Thursday. All in all, and as the days go by, they had to be among the very best that this life or any other can offer.

And so, this is the story of how I came to Meher Baba, first saw His beautiful face and came back to the home of my Beloved to place a foot in His door and make those first tentative steps across the threshold. The rest, till now, has been a case of settling in. Several years after meeting Don at Meherazad I would join the Saturday group that he oversaw in London and thus began one of the happiest periods of my life so far: working with him and our other companions on the *Neti Neti* newsletter; preparing for an assortment of seminars and events; assisting with Companion Books and then, more recently, with the Beads On One String charity that Don laid the foundations for in his latter days.

"Keep us close and keep us strong to always remember Your will be done, to love you more each and every day. Avatar Meher Baba, ki jai!"

...What is this pact you have made with Him, dear one, out of your love for us? That lets You in again and again, to always come back this way—to quicken our hearts with love and joy and lift us back into You....Sweet one, I'd thought he'd asked it of You, but now, now I'm not too sure...That it wasn't You, who pleaded with Him, out of Your infinite love for us....My 'Compassionate Father,' Avatar Meher Baba, not for nothing You have been named.

*****

At this present moment in time and place on this May Day, 2017, I find myself living in the United Kingdom; I am still involved in high school teaching (after twenty-one years), with the surface of my life experiencing a period of transition.

Meher Baba's Universal Message

I have come not to teach but to awaken. Understand therefore that I lay down no precepts.

Throughout eternity I have laid down principles and precepts, but mankind has ignored them. Man's inability to live God's words makes the Avatar's teaching a mockery. Instead of practising the compassion He taught, man has waged crusades in His name. Instead of living the humility, purity and truth of His words, man has given way to hatred, greed and violence.

Because man has been deaf to the principles and precepts laid down by God in the past, in this present Avataric Form I observe Silence. You have asked for and been given enough words—it is now time to live them. To get nearer and nearer to God you have to get further and further away from "I", "my", "me" and "mine." You have not to renounce anything but your own self. It is as simple as that, though found to be almost impossible. It is possible for you to renounce your limited self by my Grace. I have come to release that Grace.

I repeat, I lay down no precepts. When I release the tide of Truth which I have come to give, men's daily lives will be the living precept. The words I have not spoken will come to life in them.

I veil myself from man by his own curtain of ignorance, and manifest my Glory to a few. My present Avataric Form is the last Incarnation of this cycle of time, hence my Manifestation will be the greatest. When I break my Silence, the impact of my Love will be universal and all life in creation will know, feel and receive of it. It will help every individual to break himself free from his own bondage in his own way. I am the Divine Beloved who loves you more than you can ever love yourself. The breaking of my Silence will help you to help yourself in knowing your real Self.

All this world confusion and chaos was inevitable and no one is to blame. What had to happen has happened; and what has to happen will happen. There was and is no way out except through my coming in your midst. I had to come, and I have come. I am the Ancient One.

—Meher Baba

***

Avatar Meher Baba
(1894-1969)

Merwan Sheriar Irani, known as Meher baba, was born in Poona India, on February 25, 1894, of Persian parents. His father, Sheriar Irani, was of Zoroastrian faith and a true seeker of God. Merwan went to a Christian high school in Poona and later attended Deccan College. In 1913, while still in college, a momentous event occurred in his life ... the meeting with Hazrat Babajan, an ancient Muslim woman and one of the five Perfect Masters of the Age. Babajan gave him God-Realization and made him aware of his high spiritual destiny.

Eventually he was drawn to seek out another Perfect Master, Upasni Maharaj, a Hindu who lived in Sakori. During the next seven years, Maharaj gave Merwan 'gnosis,' or Divine Knowledge. Thus Merwan attained spiritual Perfection. His spiritual mission began in 1921 when he drew together his first close disciples. It was these early disciples who gave him the name Meher Baba, which means 'Compassionate Father.'

After years of intensive training of his disciples, Meher Baba established a colony near Ahmednagar that is called Meherabad. Here the Master's work embraced a free school where spiritual training was stressed, a free hospital and dispensary, and shelters for the poor. No distinction was made between the high castes and the untouchables; all mingled in common fellowship through the inspiration of the Master. To his disciples at Meherabad, who were of different castes and creeds, he gave a training of moral discipline, love for God, spiritual understanding and selfless service.

Meher Baba told his disciples that from July 10, 1925 he would observe Silence. Since that day he has maintained silence throughout the years. His many spiritual discourses and messages were dictated by means of an alphabet board. Much later the Master discontinued the use of the board and reduced all communication to hand gestures unique in expressiveness and understandable to many.

Meher Baba traveled to the Western world six times, first in 1931, when he contacted his early Western disciples. His last visit to America was in 1958, when he and his disciples stayed at the Center established for his work at Myrtle Beach, S.C.

In India, as many as one hundred thousand people have come in one day to seek his Darshan, or blessing. From all over the world there are those who journeyed to spend a few days, even a single day, in his presence.

An important part of Meher Baba's work through the years was to personally contact and to serve hundreds of those known in India as "masts." These are advanced pilgrims on the spiritual path who have become spiritually intoxicated from direct awareness of God. For this work he traveled many thousands of miles to remote places throughout India and Ceylon. Other vital work was washing of lepers, the washing of the feet of thousands of poor and distribution of grain and cloth to the destitute.

Meher Baba asserts that he is the same Ancient One, come again to redeem man from his bondage of ignorance and to guide him to realize his true Self, which is God. Meher Baba is acknowledged by his many followers all over the world as the Avatar of the Age.

Published by Meher Spiritual Center
10200 N. Kings Hwy. Myrtle Beach, SC 29572

How To Love God

To love God in the most practical way is to love our fellow beings. If we feel for others in the same way as we feel for our own dear ones, we love God.

If, instead of seeing faults in others, we look within ourselves, we are loving God.

If, instead of robbing others to help ourselves, we rob ourselves to help others, we are loving God.

If we suffer in the sufferings of others and feel happy in the happiness of others, we are loving God.

If, instead of worrying over our own misfortunes, we think of ourselves more fortunate than many many others, we are loving God.

If we endure our lot with patience and contentment, accepting it as His Will, we are loving God.

If we understand and feel that the greatest act of devotion and worship to God is not to hurt or harm any of His beings, we are loving God.

To love God as He ought to be loved, we must live for God and die for God, knowing that the goal of life is to Love God, and find Him as our own self.

Meher Baba

"I HAVE COME TO SOW THE SEED OF LOVE IN YOUR HEARTS SO THAT IN SPITE OF ALL SUPERFICIAL DIVERSITY WHICH YOUR LIFE IN ILLUSION MUST EXPERIENCE AND ENDURE, THE FEELING OF ONENESS THROUGH LOVE IS BROUGHT ABOUT AMONGST ALL NATIONS, CREEDS, SECTS AND CASTES OF THE WORLD."

Originally published by Meher Spiritual Center, Inc. 1964

GLOSSARY

aarti, arti or (in Sanskrit) arati: Song or prayer offered in devotion to God.

ahwal: (Arabic) Inner states.

Amartithi: (Hindi) January 31—the anniversary of the day Meher Baba dropped His body in 1969. Literally, "immortal date" or "deathless day."

Avatar: (Hindi) God in human form—the direct descent of God into creation.

baraka: (Arabic) Power or blessing—a byproduct of Sufi 'work.'

daaman: (Hindi) The skirt or hem of a garment.

dargah: (Persian, Urdu) A shrine built over the grave of a revered religious figure, often a Sufi saint.

darshan: (Hindi) Audience with or sight of the Master, Who bestows blessings on devotees.

dhuni: (Hindi) A sacred fire having the power of a saint.

faux pas: (French) Mistake or blunder.

firasat: (Arabic) Intuitive insight.

hal: (Arabic) A state of ecstasy in a Sama gathering.

mandali: (Sanskrit) From 'mandala,' meaning 'circle.' Members of Meher Baba's close disciples were referred to as 'mandali.'

maqbara: (Arabic) Small gravesite of a holy person.

mastur: (Arabic) Secret or hidden—a Sufi whose work does not include training murids.

maya: (Hindi) The realm of illusion.

murid: (Arabic) An aspirant or student of the Sufi way.

murshid: (Arabic) A Sufi teacher or guide.

Natraj/Natraja: (Sanskrit) The Lord of the dance. Shiva as the cosmic ecstatic dancer.

nazar: (Arabic, Turkish) Gaze, watchful eye.

Nyingma: (Tibetan) Ancient. The oldest of four major schools of Tibetan Buddhism.

Parvardigar: (Persian) Title for God. Literally, 'sustainer.'

prasad: (Hindi) prasada (Sanskrit) A small item of food, often a sweet, given to worshippers after worship.

qawwali: (Persian/Arabic) Sufi devotional music.

ramada: (Spanish) In southwestern United States, a shelter with a roof but no walls.

Sadguru: (Hindi) A Perfect Master.

sadhu: (Hindi) A pilgrim or advanced soul.

sahavas: (Hindi) A gathering of devotees in the company of the Master, that they may enjoy His physical presence.

sama: (Arabic) Audition. Sufi meetings where music and zikr are performed.

samadhi: (Hindi) A trance state brought on through spiritual meditation. The Tomb-shrine of Avatar Meher Baba.

sans: (French) qithout.

sanskaras: (Sanskrit) mental impressions affecting karma.

sanyasi: (Hindi) fourth life stage—renunciation.

Sardarji: (Hindi) A respectful appellation for a Sikh.

satchitananda: (Hindi) Representing existence, consciousness and bliss.

satsang: (Sanskrit) Sitting together with a guru or a group of spiritual students, focusing on truth.

Shri or Sri: (Sanskrit, Hindi) A title of respect used before the name of a man.

siddhis: (Hindi) Divine Powers. Also occult powers.

Sikh: (Punjab) Disciples of God who follow the writings and teachings of the Ten Sikh Gurus.

thali: (Hindi) A round plate fashioned to hold six flavors of foods.

tienda: (Spanish) Shop or store.

zazen: (Japanese) Seated meditation.

zikr: (Arabic) Remembrance of Allah by verbal repetition of names of Allah or of other phrases used by Sufis.

ziyarat: (Arabic) Visit to the tomb of a saint.

BOOKS BY MEHER BABA

Beams on the Spiritual Panorama. Essays by Baba given to the editors of God Speaks.

Discourses. Practical spirituality presented by the Source of true knowledge.

The Everything and the Nothing. Discourses for those who long for Truth.

God Speaks. All-encompassing spiritual cosmology and involution of the spirit. Mankind's journey from its origin and back to God.

Listen, Humanity. Account of "The Three Incredible Weeks," narrated and edited by Don E. Stevens at Baba's direction.

BOOKS ABOUT MEHER BABA

As Only God Can Love, by Darwin Shaw—an early American disciple's experiences with Meher Baba.

Avatar, by Jean Adriel—Meher Baba's life narrated by an early American disciple.

The God-Man, by Charles Purdom—focus on Meher Baba's journeys, work, silence.

How a Master Works, by Ivy Duce—Murshida of Sufism Reoriented recounts her experiences with Meher Baba.

The Joyous Path, by Heather Nadel—the life of Meher Baba's sister, Mani.

Lord Meher, by Bhau Kalchuri—a comprehensive account of Meher Baba's life and work in twenty volumes.

Love Alone Prevails, by Kitty Davy—an English disciple's account of life with Meher Baba in India and in the West.

Mehera-Meher, by David Fenster—the Divine Romance between Meher Baba and His chief female disciple.

Much Silence, by Tom and Dorothy Hopkinson—succinct introduction to Meher Baba.

That's How It Was, by Eruch Jessawala—heartful tales of daily life with Baba.

The Wayfarers, by William Donkin—thorough account of Meher Baba's work with masts.

Book Sources

Sheriar Books, 603 Briarwood Drive, Myrtle Beach, SC 29572
Phone: 843-272-1339   E-mail: laura@sheriarbooks.org

The Love Street Bookstore, 1214 S. Van Ness Avenue,
Los Angeles, CA 90019
Phone: 310-837-6419   E-mail: Bababook@pacbell.net

Searchlight Books, PO Box 5552, Walnut Creek, CA 94596
Phone: 925-934-9365

www.amazon.com

MEHER BABA CENTERS

Avatar Meher Baba Trust
King's Road, Post Bag 31, Ahmednagar 414-001, India
chairman@ambppct.org
www.ambppct.org
(+91) 241-2343666

The Meher Spiritual Center
10200 N. Kings Hwy, Myrtle Beach, South Carolina 29572
gateway@mehercenter.org
www.mehercenter.org
843-272-5777

Avatar Meher Baba Heartland Center
NBU 7804, 1319 Barta, Prague, OK 74864
AMB.Heartland@gmail.com
405-567-4774

Avatar Meher Baba Center of Southern California
1214 S. Van Ness Avenue, Los Angeles, CA 90019-3520
info@meherabode.org
310-731-3737

The Meher Baba Centre
228 Hammersmith Grove, London W6 7HG, UK
centre@meherbaba.co.uk
0208-743-4408

Avatar's Abode
19 Meher Road, Woombye, Qld 4559 Australia
www.avatarsabode.com.au
(617) 5442-1544

CPSIA information can be obtained
at www.ICGtesting.com
Printed in the USA
FFHW021952060419
51476413-56954FF